J. G. D. Stearns

The Meaning and Power of Baptism

J. G. D. Stearns

The Meaning and Power of Baptism

ISBN/EAN: 9783337814281

Printed in Europe, USA, Canada, Australia, Japan

Cover: Foto ©Lupo / pixelio.de

More available books at **www.hansebooks.com**

THE
MEANING AND POWER

OF

BAPTISM.

BY
REV. J. G. D. STEARNS.

Τὸ ἀλλοιωθῆναι τὸν βαπτιζόμενον.—BASIL.

NEW YORK:
N. TIBBALS & SONS, PUBLISHERS,
37 PARK ROW.
1877.

Copyright.
J. G. D. STEARNS.
1876.

CONTENTS.

CHAPTER I.
The Meaning Determined by Usage, ... 13

CHAPTER II.
Examples of Usage, ... 37

CHAPTER III.
Special Discussion of Sirach xxxiv. 30, . . . 72

CHAPTER IV.
Genuineness of the Quotation from Josephus, . . 92

CHAPTER V.
Baptisms in the Septuagint, ... 103

CHAPTER VI.
Secondary Meaning in the Lexicons, ... 123

CHAPTER VII.
Biblical Scholars, ... 133

CHAPTER VIII.
Jewish Baptisms in the New Testament, . . . 154

CHAPTER IX.
Baptism with Water, ... 180

CHAPTER X.
The Baptism of Jesus, ... 215

CHAPTER XI.
The Baptism of the Holy Ghost, ... 235

CHAPTER XII.
Baptism into Christ, ... 258

PREFACE.

OF the origin of this book some explanation is due. Controversy is not congenial to my feelings, nor consonant to my accustomed method of treating religious truth. But the incessant agitation of the subject of baptism by those who teach that there is no baptism without immersion, and, as some say, no salvation without baptism, called forth from various sources the expression of a desire that I would preach a discourse on the subject. The discourse, whose only aim was to give instruction on this as on other Biblical themes, was delivered and, by request, was printed. Some time afterwards a harsh review of the sermon appeared, to which a reply was made in "The Reviewer Reviewed." Another review came, to which a reply was contemplated; but the character of the review was such that I decided, without making formal reference to the review, to present the subject on its own merits. This will better accomplish the purpose of the book, which is not to meet the demands of those who delight in controversy, but of those who are sincerely desirous of knowing the truth. I shall not discuss the subject in all its myriad aspects, but shall treat of such points as from time to time have come up for enquiry. This explanation is given to account for the selection of the topics, as well as for the occasion of the book, and for the style and method in which it is written. The aim has been to give to all the topics treated a thorough discussion, and it is hoped that it will meet a want which is widely felt and often expressed.

CLEARWATER, MINN., *July*, 1876.

THE MEANING AND POWER OF BAPTISM.

CHAPTER I.

THE MEANING DETERMINED BY USAGE.

CHILDREN learn the meaning of their mother tongue in the daily intercourse of life. Those who spoke and wrote the Greek language in the times of the New Testament understood its meaning as well as we do our own vernacular. The Greek word BAPTIZO was in current use among the Jewish people, who had spoken the Greek language for several generations, and they were so familiar with its meaning that they needed no explanation.

The usual method in which scholars have conveyed to us the meaning of the ancient languages has been by means of lexicons, commentaries, and sometimes by dissertations or treatises on words of special importance. Another method is by giving examples of the use of words in quotations from ancient authors. This method has a signal advantage. It presents the authors themselves to our view, and gives us the opportunity to see the meaning of their words as they themselves were accustomed to use them in current speech. It allows "the impartial witnesses of antiquity to speak directly" to us, and we can judge of their meaning as we do of the words we daily read or hear. Examples will be given in the second chapter from Jewish and Patristic writers of the meaning of baptizo in its religious usage.

As this word has a classic origin, and as its classic usage sustains a relation to its religious usage, and, by the laws of language-development, prepared the way for it, and as appeal is often made to its classic usage in the interpretation of it in the New Testament, this preliminary chapter will be given to a brief consideration of its meaning in classic Greek.

The two Greek words BAPTO and BAPTIZO resemble each other in appearance and in sound, and have been "considered by most writers as perfectly identical in their signification.... The learned Dr. Gale ... says ... that they are exactly the same as to signification" (Carson on "Baptism," p. 18). But recent investigation has shown that these words differ from each other in meaning, and that they each have

The Meaning determined by Usage. 15

primary and secondary significations. A comparison of these words in respect to their differences and resemblances in classic usage will facilitate the understanding of the meaning of baptizo in Hellenistic Greek, which is the language of the New Testament.

The primary meaning of bapto, *to dip*, is illustrated in such examples as the following:

"One must dip [the bucket] and then draw it up" (Aristotle).

"Dip honey with a pitcher" (Theocritus).

"Take a vessel, and, dipping it, bring hither some sea-water" (Euripides).

"To-day . . . dip not" your pitchers in the river (Callimachus).

These are samples from an extensive usage in Greek writers, and such examples make it plain that bapto, in its primary signification, denotes entrance into a fluid, with immediate return. It is therefore represented in English by the word *dip*, which means "to put for a moment into any liquid; to insert in a fluid and withdraw again" (Webster). It denotes a definite act—*to dip*.

Until recently it has been maintained that this is the only meaning of bapto, and that baptizo has exactly the same meaning; that the two words have one and the same signification; that both words mean dip, and nothing but dip, in the whole Greek language. Dr. Gale says: "Dipping only is baptism. I'll begin with the words bapto and baptizo, for they are synonymous." Dr. F. A. Cox says: "The idea of *dipping* is *in every instance* conveyed . . . by all the current uses of the terms" (Dale, "Johannic Baptism," pp. 44, 45). The translator of the Baptist Version of Mark and Luke says: "There is no difference, as to signification, between bapto and baptizo." The translator of the Baptist Version of Acts says: "*They can have but one literal and proper meaning.* . . . Bapto occurs in the New Testament three times, always translated by *dip.*" Roger Williams, on his return from England to this country in 1644, brought over a treatise bearing the title: "Dipping is Baptizing, and Baptizing is Dipping." In the *Baptist Quarterly*, October, 1871, T. J. M. says: "It must never be forgotten that the radical idea of baptism is *a dipping into*" ("Christic and Patristic Baptism," p. 151).

But the primary meaning of bapto is not its only meaning. It has also the secondary meaning to *dye*. In its primary meaning it denotes a specific act—*to dip ;* but in its secondary meaning it does not express any specific act, but it

The Meaning determined by Usage. 17

expresses the *condition* of the object which is dyed. It does not express the act by which the quality of color is communicated to the object, but it expresses the condition of color which is produced in the object. This condition may be produced by *any* act that can bring the object under the influence of the coloring material. It may be done by dipping, or by sprinkling, or by pouring, or by any other mode that can secure the result.

"When it drops upon the garments, they are *dyed*" (Hippocrates).

In this instance the *act* by which the coloring fluid comes upon the garments is expressed by the word "drops"; but the *effect* in the colored condition of the garments is expressed by the word "*dyed*" (bapto).

"He fell, without even looking upwards, and the lake was *dyed* with blood" (Æsop).

In the battle of the frogs and mice in the fable, the blood of the champion that was killed tinged the lake with a red color. The word expresses the condition of the lake as colored by the blood.

"This garment, *dyed* by the sword of Ægisthus, is a witness to me" (Æschylus).

The blood running down over the sword gave it a red color.

"A garment *dyed* in blood" (Rev. xix. 13).

The translation "*dyed*," as given by Stuart, is correct, rather than the English version, " dipped." The garment of Him who rode on the white horse was stained with the blood of his enemies in the conflict of battle.

" The color of things *dyed* is changed by the aforesaid causes" (Aristotle).

The change in the color of things that are dyed is an *effect* of the causes that operate to produce the change, and this change of condition is expressed by the word "*dyed*."

" They are desirous to dye wool, so as to make it purple " (Plato).

The condition is changed from a white to a purple color.

" They *dye* the robe of Venus " (Achilles Tatius).

Dr. Carson accepts this secondary meaning of bapto, and admits " that *dyeing* is the secondary meaning of this word " ; that it " denotes *dyeing*, without reference to mode." " It signifies *to dye in any manner* " (" Baptism," p. 44). Dr. Dale, who has elucidated the subject more fully, says: " *Bapto, secondary, demands for its object a dyed condition*. It has no form of act of its own." " *It drops all demand for any form of act, and makes requisition only for a condition or quality* of color, satisfied with any act which will meet this requirement" ("Classic Baptism," pp. 351, 158).

The word has also other meanings—*to wet, to stain, to bedew, to gild, to moisten*, examples of which are given by Stuart and Dale. "Being pressed, it moistens and colors the hand" (Aristotle).

Here bapto, *moisten*, does not express the act of pressing the berry, but the *effect* on the hand. It does not dip the hand; it *moistens* the hand with the juice of the berry.

The admission by immersionists of a secondary meaning to bapto is very recent. It was long and earnestly maintained that bapto and baptizo are equivalent in signification. For two and a half centuries this opinion was defended. Elaborate argumentation was put forth to show that even such examples of bapto as are given above have only the primary meaning, *to dip*. Dr. Gale, a learned and eminent defender of this theory, says of the quotation from Æsop: "The literal sense is, the lake was *dipped in blood*." In explaining it he represented the lake as "dipped by hyperbole." Such inflation of rhetoric must sooner or later collapse. Even Dr. Carson exclaims: "What a monstrous paradox in rhetoric is the figure of the dipping of a lake in the blood of a mouse!" (p. 48). Since the defence of the secondary meaning by Dr. Carson, it has been more generally admitted. Alexander Campbell acknowledges that bapto signifies both *to dip* and *to dye*.

These two meanings of bapto have widely different characteristics. The primary meaning denotes a *specific act*—to dip; the secondary meaning expresses *condition*—a dyed condition. The primary meaning expresses only one kind of act—to dip; the secondary meaning admits of any one of several acts that can effect the condition. The act by which an object can be dyed may be that of putting into, dropping upon, pouring, sprinkling, pressing, smearing, or any other act that can produce the condition of color in the object. The act denoted by bapto primary is a *momentary* act, transient, feeble in its influence; the condition which bapto secondary expresses is *permanent:* it has no limit of time.

As the meaning of bapto has been determined by an appeal to usage, so the meaning of baptizo can be determined by a similar appeal. The argument of Dr. Carson from the derivation of the word, in which he is followed by Alexander Campbell and others, is in itself of no force, and has no value unless sustained by usage. Alexander Campbell says that "baptizo indicates a *specific* action, and can have but one meaning; it derives its meaning and immutable form from bapto, and therefore inherits the proper meaning of the *bap*, which is *dip*" ("Christic and Patristic Baptism," p. 18). But, as Dr. Carson says, p. 46: "USE IS THE SOLE ARBITER OF LANGUAGE." It is in the actual usage of the word that its meaning is seen. Examples of usage are decisive, while derivation, even if ascertained, cannot be decisive; for, if bapto can undergo a change of meaning by usage, baptizo can also receive a meaning from usage different from its root.

Before the two meanings of bapto and baptizo were distinguished from each other, the supposition that baptizo was derived from bapto was relied upon as evidence that the two words were perfectly identical in signification. But bapto has two meanings, a primary and a secondary. From which of these two meanings does baptizo come? Does it come from bapto primary, which denotes a specific act? Or does it come from bapto secondary, which expresses condition resulting from any act competent to effect the condition? And if it comes from the one or the other, whichever it be, has the derivative the same identical meaning as its primitive? Are two words needed to express one and the same identical meaning? "Baptist writers say it comes from *bapto, to dip*. They once said bapto did not mean *to dye*; they now admit that it does. But they have not reviewed the meaning of *baptizo* in the light of this correction" (Dale). The question returns, Does baptizo come from bapto primary, which denotes a specific act, "mode and nothing but mode"? (Carson). Or does it come from bapto secondary, which "*drops all demand for any form of act, and makes requisition only for condition,* . . . satisfied with any act which will meet the requirement"? (Dale). Dr. Carson affirms the former, Dr. Dale the latter. Dr. Carson, "American Baptist Publication Society," 1860, p. 55. says: "*Bapto*, the root, I have shown to possess two meanings, and two only: *to dip* and *to dye*. *Baptizo*, I have asserted, has but one signification. It has been formed on the idea of the primary meaning of the root, and has never admitted the secondary. . . . My position is THAT IT ALWAYS SIGNIFIES TO DIP, NEVER EXPRESSING ANYTHING BUT MODE."

Dr. Dale, on the other hand, says: "For this statement there is not the shadow of support, as seen by the facts of usage and the defining terms of lexicographers. The reverse statement would be far nearer the truth. There is no evidence that baptizo does ever give expression to dip in its specific character. There is no evidence that it expresses modal act of any kind. There is no conclusive evidence that 'this word has been formed on the primary meaning of the root.' There is, I think, conclusive evidence to the contrary. It is incredible that a second word should be created which was to be the simple *ditto* of one already existing. The whole history of the word declares that what was *à priori* incredible has, in reality, no existence. . . . On the other hand, the general characteristics of the secondary meaning of the root appear in the boldest relief through all the history of the word. I say the general characteristics," not "the specialty of bapto *second* in the direction of *dyeing, staining, coloring,* etc. . . . Baptizo is an extension of bapto *second* (the *dyeing* excluded), with all its rights and privileges as to freedom of act and rejection of envelopment, and advancing to give full development to characteristic qualities, powers and influences over appropriate objects. . . . This view harmonizes with that of grammarians who derive baptizo from baptos, a derivative from bapto second" ("Johannic Baptism," p. 64).

The opinion that baptizo is "formed on the primary meaning" of bapto has no reason for its support. Two words of the same identical meaning in one language are not needed; and as one good word was already in use in the Greek language to signify dip, it is, as Dale says, "incredible" that another word should be created to signify exactly the same thing. Instead of creating several words to express one meaning, we find that one word has several meanings in numerous instances in all languages.

The actual meaning of baptizo can be determined only *by its usage;* and in its usage it has the characteristics of the secondary meaning of the root. It does not belong to that class of verbs "which make demand for a definite act to be done," but to that large class which "make demand for an effect, a state, or a condition to be accomplished" ("Classic Baptism," p. 106). Dr. James W. Dale, who has given this word the most thorough investigation which it has received from any man, in the four volumes which contain the result of his examination of the usage of the word—Classic, Judaic, Johannic, Christic and Patristic Baptism—has demonstrated that the word baptizo does not denote a specific act, as *to dip, to sprinkle, to pour,* but it expresses *con-*

The Meaning determined by Usage. 25

dition resulting from some competent act. It thus differs essentially from the primary meaning of bapto, and resembles the secondary meaning in its general characteristics. "Bapting is not baptizing, nor is baptizing bapting."

In classic usage baptizo has both primary and secondary meanings. As the secondary meaning which it has in Hellenistic Greek will be fully illustrated in the second chapter, it will be sufficient here to give a brief statement of its meaning in classic usage, with a few examples in illustration.

BAPTIZO DENOTES A CHANGE IN THE CONDITION OF ITS OBJECT, THE NATURE OF THE CHANGE BEING DETERMINED BY THE NATURE OF THE BAPTIZING POWER.

1. Baptizo expresses a change in the condition of its object. The vital idea in a baptism is a thorough change in the character, state, or condition of its object. There are many baptisms of a diverse nature, but this is the ground idea common to all baptisms.

2. Baptizo expresses condition, but not the act by which the condition is effected. It implies some act or agency, but the act is not expressed by the word itself, but is otherwise expressed or left unexpressed. It accepts of any act or of any

influence that is competent to effect the condition. It expresses a condition of stupor caused by the act of swallowing an opiate, a condition of drunkenness caused by drinking wine, a condition of coldness caused by pouring cold water on hot iron, a condition of purity by the use of pure water in any way. The acts and agencies from which the diverse conditions of baptism result are very numerous, and their modes of operation are diverse. More than fifty baptismal agencies appear in the works of Dale. Dr. Conant, in his translation of the word, gives no less than forty different acts by which baptisms are effected ("Classic Baptism,' p. 74).

3. Baptizo, in its primary meaning, expresses *inness* of condition. The object is in a state of *intusposition*—*i.e.*, position within a fluid, a semi-solid, or a solid. Aristotle speaks of "certain desert places full of rush and sea-weed, which, when it is ebb tide, are not baptized, but, when it is full tide, are flooded " ("Classic Baptism," p. 236). The sea-coast is not taken up and dipped into the ocean. The tide, rising up, overflows it. The baptism was its condition under the water. Strabo says: "The army marched throughout the entire day baptized up to the waist." The

act was marching. The baptism was the condition of the soldiers on the march. Plotinus and other Greek writers speak of "the soul baptized by the body" ("Classic Baptism," p. 264). A corporeal body is the investing element; but how the soul becomes enclosed in the body, the mode of this baptism, would be a question extraneous to the meaning of the word.

4. Baptizo expresses condition without limit of duration. It expresses the condition of its object within the investing element for an indefinite period of time. In this as in other respects it differs radically from bapto primary, which expresses *momentary* continuance in the fluid, denoting entrance into a fluid with immediate return. Baptizo does not take out what it puts in, but leaves its object in the element into which it introduces it. Some other agency may withdraw the object, but baptizo never does. Ships baptized—*i.e.*, sunk in the sea—remain in that condition.

"Our vessel having been baptized in the midst of the Adriatic" (Josephus).

"His ship having been baptized" (Diodorus Siculus).

"They made incessant attacks, and baptized many of the ships" (Polybius).

"A lofty billow rising above baptized them" (Josephus).

Nearly thirty examples occur in Greek writers of the baptism of ships. The act by which the baptism of the ships is caused is not that of dipping —putting them into the water for a moment and taking them out. The ships sink to the bottom, and *remain* in that condition of baptism for ages. The duration of this baptism has not yet run out. It still continues after the lapse of two thousand years.

Animals, and also men, are in like manner baptized. "Many of the land animals, enclosed by the river, perish, being baptized" (Diodorus Siculus).

The animals were not dipped. The water flowed over them by the inundation of the river Nile, and they came permanently under its suffocating power.

"The river, rolling down with a stronger current, baptized many, and destroyed them" (Diodorus Siculus).

In this baptism the soldiers were not dipped. A mere dipping could not have injured them. They were baptized—*i.e.*, they were brought under the watery element, and *remained* under it. It was a death-baptism by drowning.

The Meaning determined by Usage.

"Being baptized by the Galatians in a pool, according to command, he died" (Josephus).

"Thrust such an one on the head, baptizing him, so that he can rise no more" (Timon, the Man-hater, in Lucian).

"The dolphin, displeased at such a falsehood, baptizing, killed him" (Æsop).

"Baptizing you by sea-waves, I will destroy you" (Alcibiades; "Classic Baptism," p. 266).

"I found Cupid among the roses, and, holding him by the wings, I baptized him into the wine, and took and drank him" (Julian, Egypt.; "Classic Baptism," p. 245).

He was not dipped—put in and taken out. He remained in the wine, and in that condition was swallowed by the drinker.

"When the sons of the prophet were cutting wood with axes over the river Jordan, the iron fell off and was baptized in the river" (Justin Martyr; "Judaic Baptism," p. 252).

This baptism of the axe would have lasted to the end of time but for a miracle. The condition of baptism has no self-termination. Baptism of itself never recovers its object from the condition in which it places it. This is now admitted. The *National Baptist* says: "Dr. Dale has brought clearly out what our examination had before proved, that the word baptizo does not of itself involve the lifting out from the fluid of that which is put in." The *Baptist Quarterly*, April, 1869, says: "Our Lord did not command *to put people into the water and take them out again, but to put them under the water.* . . . That baptizo *never* does engage to take its subject out of the water . . . we readily admit" ("Judaic Baptism," pp. 25, 49).

Dr. Conant, BAPTIZEIN, ed. 1868, p. 88, after saying that "the word immerse expresses the full import of the Greek word *baptizein*," adds: "The idea of *emersion* is not included in the meaning of the Greek word. It means, simply, to put into or under water." Then the word baptizo does not mean *dip;* for that, in Hebrew, Latin, Greek, and English, always *does* take out what it puts in. If the idea of putting in and taking out is to be expressed in classic Greek, baptizo does not express it. It is the Greek word bapto, and not baptizo, which those who spoke and wrote the Greek language employed to denote the definite act *to dip*. They employed the word baptizo to express the permanent condition of the object under the water where it placed it. We must look elsewhere than to the classic usage of baptizo for a reason to take people out of the

The Meaning determined by Usage. 31

water. "The instinctive love of life will do it," it is said. True, indeed! But this is an influence *outside* of the Greek word baptizo.

5. Baptizo, like innumerable words in all languages, has a *secondary* meaning, and, in its secondary use, it expresses condition resulting from causes *without* intusposition in water, or in any other element. An opiate *drunk* from *a cup* baptizes—*i.e.*, brings into a condition of stupor (Achilles Tatius;" C. B.," p. 318). Wine drunk from a cup baptizes, brings into a state of drunkenness (Conon;" C. B.," p. 317). Drinking from the Silenic fount baptizes, makes one heavy-headed and dull (Lucian; "C. B.," p. 330). Water poured into wine baptizes, dilutes, tempers the wine, thus changing its condition (Plutarch; "C. B.," p. 339). Puzzling questions put to a boy in school baptize him, put him into a condition of bewilderment (Plato; "C. B.," p. 334). In these and countless other Greek baptisms there is no immersion. The persons baptized, and the various other objects of baptism, are not dipped into the element. The subjects of the opiate-baptism were not dipped into the cup. They drank the baptizing element from the cup.

6. Baptizo, both in its primary and in its secondary use, *secures the influence* of the baptizing ele-

ment over the object baptized. Unlike bapto primary, which expresses only a transient act of feeble influence, *baptizo is a word of* POWER. This idea of power originates in the primary use of the word. The starting point is the condition of intusposition for a long, indefinite period in which baptizo places its objects. As the object which baptizo puts into the water or other investing element remains in the element and is not withdrawn, the baptizing element has time to exert its full influence upon the object encompassed by it. Some objects, like flint, or the iron in the axe-baptism of Justin Martyr, receive no perceptible influence from the surrounding medium. But most objects do receive an influence from the enveloping element. Complete envelopment in a fluid, a semi-solid, or a solid will, in time, develop its full influence over the object which comes under its power. The object receives the quality of the baptizing element, and is thus changed in its condition. A bag of salt in water dissolves. A sponge in water imbibes the element and is drenched. Ships sunk in the sea gradually undergo change by the constant action of the water. Men and animals encompassed by the watery element are suffocated. Fruit baptized in brine receives the quality of the brine and is changed to pickle (Nicander; "C. B.," p. 273). Objects enclosed in marsh mud are by it changed in the course of time. The soul baptized in the body develops and receives "the oppressive, sensuous influence of the body." Objects remaining enclosed in the baptizing element for years and for ages receive more than a dipping. They come under the controlling influence of the fluid or solid elements that enclose them. The encompassing element penetrates the object which it surrounds, and pervades it with its own peculiar influence, and changes its condition. Thus by usage baptizo becomes a word expressing *a thorough change in the condition* of its object by the *controlling influence* of the baptizing element.

In its secondary use, also, baptizo develops and secures the influence of the baptizing agency over the baptized object. There is no immersion in secondary baptism. Intusposition disappears; but those baptizing agencies which operate without intusposition exert their own peculiar influence over the baptized objects. The opiate drug has a powerful influence in baptizing the man who drinks it. It penetrates his system and produces a condition of stupefaction. The resemblance between primary and secondary baptism consists in the idea of *influence* which is common to both. Intusposition is eliminated in secondary use. There is no immersion, no enclosing medium, no receptive element into which the object baptized is introduced, no encompassing fluid or solid, as in primary baptism, but the resemblance is in the influence which the baptismal agencies exert over the objects which come under their control. In both classes of baptisms, primary and secondary, the baptismal agencies exert each its own peculiar influence, and the nature of the baptism corresponds.

In both primary and secondary baptisms, the *character of the change* in the baptized object corresponds to *the nature of the baptizing power*. The baptizing agency communicates its own characteristic quality to the object which it baptizes, and assimilates it to its own nature. Each baptizing agency exerts its own specific influence upon the object which it baptizes. Water enveloping a living man penetrates and pervades his system, and by its peculiar influence over him produces suffocation. Ships penetrated by the water of the surrounding ocean become subject to its influence.

So the opiate drop, in baptizing the man who drinks it, communicates to him its stupefying influence and puts him to sleep. Wine drunk from a cup penetrates and pervades the human system, and baptizes the man by communicating to him its intoxicating influence. The alcoholic quality baptizes him, makes him drunk. There are numerous examples of these wine-baptisms in Greek writers, extending through a period of more than a thousand years. The specific influence of each baptizing agency on the character of its objects corresponds to the characteristic quality of that agency. Some baptismal agencies have purifying qualities, and these purifying qualities give them a special influence in the service of religion. A baptized man is a man brought into a baptized condition by some baptizing agency, and the character of the baptism corresponds to the characteristic quality of the baptizing power. The special influence of those baptismal agencies which, from their purifying qualities, are employed for religious purposes, will be illustrated in the next chapter.

What has thus far been said is only preparatory to the main question respecting the religious signification of the word. It is no inconsiderable advantage to distinguish between bapto and baptizo, which have been so long confounded, and to illustrate the principle on which the argument from usage in the next chapter will proceed. The

Hellenistic usage rests upon a classic foundation. Even the secondary meaning—purification—has an illustration in Plutarch ("C. B.," p. 342). But the Hellenistic meaning has an ample illustration in its own sphere. This meaning will be determined by examples of usage, in confident reliance upon the principle which Dr. Dale has applied with such eminent success, that "USE IS OF SUPREME AUTHORITY AND THE RULE IN THE LANGUAGE."

CHAPTER II.

EXAMPLES OF USAGE—JEWISH BAPTISMS.

THE Patrists call the purifications under the Law baptisms; and these baptisms they represent as typical of baptism under the Gospel. The baptismal agencies were sacrificial blood, heifer-ashes, and water; the mode of applying them was by sprinkling; and the baptism resulting was a condition of ceremonial purification. A few examples will illustrate this.

1. Ambrose, in commenting on the Septuagint of Ps. l. 9, "Sprinkle me with hyssop, and I shall be clean; wash me, and I shall be whiter than snow," calls the purification a baptism: "He asks to be cleansed by hyssop according to the Law; he desires to be washed according to the Gospel. He who wished to be cleansed by typical baptism was sprinkled with the blood of the lamb by a bunch of hyssop" ("Christic and Patristic Baptism," p. 534).

In the baptism which Ambrose thus describes, the baptismal agency was the blood of the sacrificial lamb, the means of applying it to the person was a hyssop-branch, the mode was by sprinkling, the baptism resulting was a condition of ceremonial purification ; and this baptism was a type of baptism under the Gospel.

2. Ambrose: " He who is baptized, whether in conformity with the Law or in conformity with the Gospel, is cleansed: in conformity with the Law, because Moses sprinkled the blood of the lamb with a bunch of hyssop ; in conformity with the Gospel, because the raiment of Christ was white as snow. . . . ' Therefore he is white as snow whose sins are forgiven " ("Judaic Baptism," p. 188).

Baptism under the Law and under the Gospel is purification, and Ambrose identifies these baptisms as type and antitype baptisms.

3. Basil : " The blood of the lamb is a type of the blood of Christ " (p. 217).

4. Hilary : " *Sprinkling* according to the Law was the cleansing of sin, through faith purifying the people by the *sprinkling* of blood (Ps. l. 9) ; a sacrament of the future *sprinkling* of the blood of the Lord" (" The Baptism of Calvary," p. 34).

5. Didymus Alexandrinus, teacher of the most renowned Greek school of his age, says : " The very image of baptism both continually illuminated and saved all Israel at that time, as Paul

wrote (1 Cor. x. 1, 2), and as prophesied Ezekiel (xxxvi. 25): 'I will sprinkle clean water upon you, and you shall be clean from all your sins'; and David (Ps. l. 9): 'Sprinkle me with hyssop, and I shall be clean.' For the *sprinkling* with hyssop was Judaic purification, which is continued to the present time; but 'whiter than snow' denotes Christian illumination, which means baptism." He further compares the "baptism which was formerly *in shadow*' with "that which is *in reality*," which he calls "the antitype baptism" ("Jud. Bap.," p. 196; "C. and P. B.," p. 342).

6. Cyril, Archbishop of Alexandria, on Isaiah, Book I. Dis. I., referring the expression (i. 16), "Wash you, make you clean," to baptism, says: "And this the ancient law imaged forth to them as in shadows, and preached before the grace which is through the holy baptism. For he said (Num. viii. 6, 7): 'Take the Levites and cleanse them. And thus shalt thou do to cleanse them: Sprinkle water of purifying upon them'" (Conant, p. 123; Beecher, p. 164).

7. Ambrose: "The Lord also commanded Moses that if any leprous person would be cleansed. . . . Whoever wished to be cleansed in proper form was sprinkled by these three; because no one can be cleansed from the leprosy

of sin by the water of baptism except under the invocation of the Father, and of the Son, and of the Holy Ghost. . . . And he cleanses us, who are designated by the leper, by their invocation and by the water of baptism " ("Jud. Bap.," p. 185).

In thus interpreting Jewish baptism in cleansing the leper as emblematical of Christian baptism, Ambrose again teaches that the essential nature of baptism under the Law and under the Gospel is a condition of purification.

8. Cyril, Archbishop of Jerusalem, in his address to the candidates for baptism, says: " Rejoice, O heavens! and be glad, O earth! because of those who are about to be sprinkled with hyssop, and to be purified by the spiritual hyssop, through the power of Him who drank, in his suffering, from the hyssop and the reed " (p. 188).

Cyril speaks of the rite of baptism, which he was about to administer, in the same terms that describe Jewish baptisms. The resemblance which he traced between Jewish and Christian baptism did not consist in the act or mode, but in the essential nature, of the baptism, which was a condition of purification.

BAPTISM BY HEIFER-ASHES.

1. Sirach, xxxiv. 30, more than 200 B.C., speaking of the purification from the defilement caused by touching a dead body, calls the purification a baptism: "Being baptized from a dead body, and touching it again, what is he benefited by his cleansing?" ("Jud. Bap.," p. 112).

This purification is described in Numbers, chapter xix., as a purification effected by sprinkling the ashes of a heifer on the person ceremonially defiled.

2. Josephus, "Jewish Antiquities," IV. iv. 6: "Those, therefore, defiled by a dead body, introducing a little of the ashes and hyssop-branch into a spring, and baptizing of this ashes [introduced] into the spring, they sprinkled both on the third and seventh of the days" ("Jud. Bap.," p. 100).

3. Cyril of Alexandria, in his comment on Isa. iv. 4, says: "The Creator and Lord of all, who is abundant in mercy, . . . will wash away the filth of the transgressors, and will thoroughly cleanse the blood from their midst by the spirit of judgment and the spirit of burning. . . . We call the spirit of burning the grace at the holy baptism begotten within us not with-

out the Spirit; for, indeed, *we have not been* BAPTIZED *by bare water, nor yet by the ashes of a heifer,* (since we have been sprinkled for the purification of the flesh only, according to the saying of the blessed Paul), *but by the Holy Spirit and by the divine and spiritual fire"* (Dale, MS.)

The punctuation of this passage is that of Cyril's Greek text as given by the Abbé Migne, of Paris. In this passage Cyril speaks of *three baptisms,* differing from each other as the agencies by which they were effected were different. *The first* baptism is by mere or bare water; *the second,* by heifer-ashes; *the third,* by the conjoint agency of the Holy Spirit and the divine and spiritual fire.

4. Gregory Nazianzen: " Therefore let us be baptized, that we may overcome; let us partake of the purifying waters, more purging than hyssop, more purifying than the blood of the Law, more sanctifying than the ashes of a heifer sprinkling the unclean, and having, for the time, power for the purification of the body, but not for the complete removal of sin" ("Jud. Bap.," p. 188).

In the comparison which this Greek writer makes between the Jewish purifications by sprinkling sacrificial blood and heifer-ashes and the baptism of Christianity, he teaches that the former only purifies the body ceremonially, while the latter is superior, more purifying, a purification of the most complete character.

5. Cyril of Alexandria: "The ancient law . . . preached the grace in the holy baptism. For He said (Num. viii. 6, 7): 'Take the Levites, and cleanse them. And thus shalt thou do to cleanse them: Sprinkle water of purifying upon them.' What the water of purifying is the most wise Paul shall teach, saying: 'The ashes of a heifer sprinkling the unclean sanctifieth to the purifying of the flesh.'"

This passage is repeated here because Cyril represents purification by sprinkling the ashes of a heifer as one of the things in the ancient law which give a shadow or type of baptism.

DIRECT ASSERTIONS.

The Patrists teach by direct assertion that baptism signifies purification.

1. Athanasius: "'He shall baptize you by the Holy Ghost.' This means that he will purify you" ("C. and P. B.," p. 600).

This is a direct assertion of this Greek writer that baptism means purification.

2. Clemens Romanus: "I am fully persuaded that the holy baptism of Christ is spiritual purification and regeneration both of soul and body" (p. 597).

3. Theophylact: "He calls his death a baptism, as being a purging of us all" ("Jud. Bap.," p. 217).

4. Basil the Great: "What is the purport and power of baptism? The baptized is thoroughly changed as to thought and word and deed, and becomes, according to the power bestowed, the same as that by which he was born" ("C. and P. B.," p. 491).

Basil defines baptism as a thorough change in the spiritual condition of the baptized, by which his character is assimilated to the nature of the baptizing agency. He says nothing of dipping or of any other act. Baptism is a change in the character of its object, the nature of the change being determined by the nature of the baptizing power.

5. Hippolytus: "As Isaiah says, 'Wash ye.' Dost thou see, beloved, how the prophet declared beforehand the purifying character of this baptism?" ("Jud. Bap.," p. 278).

6. Gregory Nazianzen, on Baptism, says: "But we being twofold, I mean spiritual and corporeal; . . . purification is also twofold, by water and

Spirit, . . . the one typical, the other real, and purifying the depths" ("C. and P. B.," p. 342).

7. Basil the Great: "There are three meanings of baptism: purification from defilement, regeneration by the Spirit, and trial by the fire of judgment" ("Jud. Bap.," p. 249).

Each of these three baptisms is a change of condition corresponding to the nature of the baptizing power. Purification is a condition of purity, regeneration a condition of new spiritual life, and trial by the fire of judgment a test of our condition to enter Paradise.

8. Clemens Alexandrinus: "Being baptized, we are illuminated. . . . This is variously designated. . . . It is called washing because we are cleansed from our sins" ("C. and P. B.," p. 553).

9. Theophylact, in his comment on Luke xi. 38: "He marvelled that he was not first baptized before dinner," says: "Jesus, deriding their foolish custom—I mean their purifying themselves before eating—teaches that they ought to purify their souls by good works" (Dr. E. Beecher, p. 222).

10. Theophylact, on John iii. 25, says: "Disputing concerning purification—*i.e.*, baptism—they came to their Master" (pp. 214, 221).

BAPTISM BY THE EXTENDED HAND.

1. John of Damascus: "John was baptized by putting his hand upon the divine head of his Master" ("Johannic Baptism," p. 220).

This baptism was effected by the touch of the hand. The baptismal virtue was thus conveyed from Jesus to John.

2. Hippolytus: "He bowed his head to be baptized by John" (p. 222).

The act of bowing the head to receive baptism is customary among all except immersionists.

3. Gregory Thaumaturgus: "The Baptist having heard these things, stretching out his trembling hand, baptized the Lord" (p. 405).

BAPTISM OF TEARS.

1. Clemens Alexandrinus: "He wept bitterly. . . . Having been baptized a second time by his tears" ("C. and P. B.," p. 514).

Clement is speaking of the captain of a band of robbers, once a disciple of the Apostle John, and he calls his restoration a baptism of tears. His second baptism was *a thorough change in the spiritual condition of his soul* through penitential sorrow for his sin. In this baptism a dipping is impossible. It would exhaust the lachrymal fountains of many men to furnish a sufficient quantity of tears to immerse a single individual.

2. Gregory Nazianzen: "And I know yet a fifth baptism, that by means of tears, . . . washing nightly his bed with tears" (p. 507).

The bed was not dipped in tears, neither was the penitent man, weeping on account of his sins. His penitential sorrow was a purification of the soul, a thorough change of his character, state, or condition.

3. Athanasius: "A sixth baptism is that by tears, which is painful, as one washing nightly his couch and repenting" (p. 514).

The baptism was the change of character by repentance.

4. Athanasius: "God has granted to the nature of man three baptisms purifying from all sin whatsoever. I mean . . . *third*, the baptism by tears into which the harlot was purified. And likewise Peter, the chief of the holy Apostles, after his denial, having wept, was received and saved" (p. 514).

Peter was not dipped in water when he wept over his denial of his Master. His baptism of tears was his repentance—a change in his spiritual character. This Greek writer thus expressly teaches that this baptism was a purification, and both of his examples illustrate this signification.

BAPTISM IN ONE'S OWN BLOOD.

No man can be dipped in his own blood. By the baptism of blood the Patrists mean purification.

1. Basil Magnus: "There are some who, in striving for piety, have undergone death for Christ, . . . needing for salvation nothing of the water-symbols, being baptized by their own blood" ("Johannic Baptism," p. 225).

Basil did not believe water-baptism essential to salvation. He calls it a symbol. He believed a man can be baptized in his own blood. He believed men can be saved by the baptism of blood.

2. Cyril of Jerusalem: "The Saviour redeeming the world by the cross, and wounded in his side, shed forth water and blood; that some, in times of peace, might be baptized with water, and others, in times of persecution, might be baptized with their own blood" (p. 224).

There was no dipping in this baptism. A man cannot be dipped in his own blood. His body cannot be covered over with his own blood. There is not blood enough in a man to immerse him in it. In this baptism a dipping is impossible.

3. John of Damascus: "John was baptized . . . also by his own blood" (p. 223).

We know how this baptism was effected. His head was severed from his body by order of Herod. He was not dipped in his blood; he was beheaded.

4. Jerome: "Thou dost baptize me with water, that I may baptize thee, for myself, with thy blood" (p. 228).

5. Tertullian: "Because he would teach men to be baptized not only by water, but also by their own blood; so that, baptized by this baptism only, they may secure a true faith and a pure cleansing, and, baptized in the one way or in the other, equally to secure one baptism of salvation and honor" ("C. and P. B.," p. 38).

Thus Tertullian teaches that baptism is a cleansing, and that blood-baptism and water-baptism are one baptism, which shows that dipping was not the idea in his mind, but spiritual condition.

6. Augustine teaches that even in a bloody death there is no baptism unless the character of

the person is duly changed. " If all who are slain are baptized by their blood, all robbers, unjust and impious persons who are put to death must be reckoned martyrs, because they are baptized by their own blood."

This, he says, cannot be. "If none are baptized by their own blood but those who are slain for righteousness . . ." The baptism depends upon the character of the person slain. It does not depend upon the quantity of blood in his veins, or on the possibility of dipping him in his own blood. If it did, a robber might be baptized in his blood as well as a martyr, which Augustine denies. The reality of the martyr-baptism depends on the spiritual condition of the person who suffers death. " If you die as a sacrilegious person, how are you baptized with your blood?" p. 40).

7. Bassillius, speaking of the forty martyrs, says: "They were baptized, not with water, but with their own blood" ("Baptismal Question," p. 104).

8. Cyprian: "The Lord declares that those baptized with their own blood obtain divine grace, when he says to the thief on the cross in his very Passion that 'he should be with him in Paradise'" ("C. and P. B.," p. 510).

The baptism of the thief on the cross was not

a dipping. He was not dipped in his own blood. He was nailed to the cross. By his faith in the divine Redeemer he obtained divine grace in his crucifixion-baptism.

9. Cyprian: "Can the power of baptism be greater or better than *confession*, than *martyrdom*, when one confesses Christ before men, and is baptized by his own blood?" ("Johannic Baptism," p. 227).

10. Origen: "If God would grant to me that I might be cleansed by my own blood, that I might attain that second baptism dying for Christ, I would depart out of this world secure" ("Jud. Bap.," p. 197).

Dying for Christ was the martyr-baptism, and this baptism consisted in being cleansed.

11. Jerome: "That ye should be baptized by my blood by the washing of regeneration, which alone can remit sin" ("C. and P. B.," p. 512).

12. Athanasius: "God hath granted to the nature of man three baptisms purifying from all manner of sin; I refer to that which is through water, and again that which is through our own martyr-blood, and, third, that which is through tears" (p. 42).

The three baptisms here described are purifications, and the baptismal agencies instrumental in effecting these baptisms are water, martyr-blood, and tears.

CHRIST'S BLOOD-BAPTISM.

The baptism of Christ on the cross was the central baptism in which all other Bible baptisms meet. It was a purification by atonement for the sins of mankind.

1. Gregory Nazianzen: "And I know a fourth baptism—that by means of martyrdom and blood, with which, also, Christ himself was baptized, and, indeed, much more admirable than the others" ("C. and P. B.," p. 507).

Agency, and not mode, is here expressed.

2. Petilianus: "The Saviour himself, also, having been first baptized by John, declared that he must be baptized a second time—not now by water nor by Spirit, but by the baptism of blood, by the cross of his Passion" (p. 40).

The blood was the baptizing agency in his baptism on the cross.

3. John of Damascus: "The baptism through blood and martyrdom with which Christ was baptized for us" (p. 43).

The Saviour's baptism was vicarious. He was baptized, not for himself, but for us.

4. Theophylact: "He calls his death a baptism,

Examples of Usage. 53

as being a purification for us all" (Cremer, p. 105).

The baptism of Christ on the cross was on our account. It is called a baptism, not because it was a dipping, but a purification. Jesus was not immersed on the cross, but he was baptized. This is a direct assertion of this Greek writer that the baptism of Christ on the cross was a purification.

5. Origen: "The Lord says: 'I have a baptism to be baptized with. . . .' You see that he called the pouring out of his blood, baptism" ("C. and P. B.," p. 41).

Not immersion in his blood, but the *pouring out* of his blood (*profusionem sanguinis sui* BAPTISMA .

6. Tertullian: "These two baptisms he shed forth from the wound of his pierced side" (p. 510).

The idea that Jesus was immersed either in the water or in the blood that flowed from the wound in his side is, of course, wholly inadmissible.

7. Jerome: "That ye should be baptized by my blood, which alone can remit sin" (p. 512).

It was the sin-remitting power of Christ's blood which gave it its virtue and efficacy.

8. Tertullian: "Martyrdom will be another

baptism. For He says (Luke xii. 50): 'I have also another baptism.' Whence from the wounded side of the Lord water and blood flowed forth, providing each washing: . . . first, washing by water; second, by blood" (p. 510).

Here we have Tertullian's own explanation of both of the baptisms. The water and the blood are two baptismal agencies, each of which effects a cleansing. The mode has nothing whatever to do with the nature of the baptism.

9. Petilianus: "Blush, O persecutors! ye make martyrs like to Christ, whom [quos], after the water of true baptism, baptizing blood sprinkles" (p. 40).

The baptismal virtue is in the blood. The blood of Christ has an atoning efficacy, a sin-remitting power, and the sprinkling of this blood baptizes, cleanses from sin.

10. Origen: "Christ, whom we follow, shed his blood for our redemption, that we may depart washed by our own blood. For it is the baptism of blood only which can make us purer than the baptism of water has made us" (p. 41).

The baptism of water is a purification. The baptism of blood is a more complete purification. And this cleansing comes to us through the baptism of Christ on the cross, which was a purification for us. The idea of a covering of the body either with water or with the blood that flowed from the Saviour's side is no part of the baptism. The baptism is an effect produced by these agencies, a purification for our sins. Christ's baptism on the cross was "a baptism into penal death," an atonement for the sins of mankind.

THE BAPTISM OF FIRE.

One of the effects of fire arises from its purifying efficacy. This purification by fire the Patrists call baptism.

1. Ambrose: "There is also a baptism at the entrance of Paradise which formerly did not exist; but after the transgressor was excluded, the flaming sword began to be, which was not before when sin was not. Sin began and baptism began, by which they might be purified who desired to return" ("Jud. Bap.," p. 223).

2. Origen: "Physicians say that to cure certain diseases not only is the cutting by a knife necessary, but burning, also. . . . Our sin is a cancer for which neither cutting nor burning, alone, is sufficient; both are needed. . . . Therefore the Saviour uses both sword and

fire, and baptizes those sins which could not be purged by the purification of the Holy Spirit" ("C. and P. B.," 595).

The only possible meaning of the word "baptizes" here is *purifies, cleanses*.

3. Ambrose: "Who is it that baptizes by this fire? . . . Therefore the great Baptist [*baptista*, purifier] . . . shall come, and shall see many standing at the entrance of Paradise, and shall wave the sword turning every way. . . . Therefore consuming fire must come and burn up in us the lead of iniquity, the iron of transgression, and make us pure gold" (p. 520).

4. Basil the Great: "Baptized by the fire—that is, by the word of doctrine" ("Johannic Baptism," p. 201).

Basil, by his definition of this fire-baptism, makes it, not a dipping into the fire, but an effect of the instrumentality of the fire—that is, the doctrine.

5. Jerome: "Happy is he who receives the cleansing of the Holy Spirit, and does not need the cleansing of fire. But wretched and worthy of weeping is he who, after the cleansing of the Spirit, must be baptized by fire" (p. 201).

6. Macarius Ægyptus: "The baptism of fire

and of Spirit purifies and cleanses the polluted mind " (p. 207).

7. Gregory Thaumaturgus: " Christ says to John: 'Baptize me, who am about to baptize those who believe, *through* water, and the Spirit, and fire '—*by water*, which is able to wash away the filth of sin ; *by the Spirit*, who can make the earthly spiritual ; *by fire*, whose nature it is to burn up the thorns of sin " (p. 207).

Water, Spirit, and fire are agencies by which the purification is accomplished.

8. Gregory Nazianzen: "And there is a final baptism hereafter, when they will be baptized by means of fire, both more painful and more protracted " (" C. and P. B.," p. 507).

This baptism is not a mere momentary act, a dipping into the fire ; it is a condition or state of long, indefinite duration.

9. Athanasius: " The eighth baptism is the final baptism, which is not saving, but burning and punishing sinners for ever and ever " (p. 507).

This is a destructive baptism, a condition which has no termination.

HAND-WASHING BAPTISM.

1. Clemens Alexandrinus : " Purity is to think

purely. An image of this baptism was communicated to the poets, from Moses, thus:

"'Having washed, and being clothed with clean
    vestments,
Penelope comes to prayer.'
'But Telemachus . . .
Having washed his hands of the hoary sea,
    prays to Minerva.'

"This is a custom of the Jews to baptize often upon the couch. Therefore it is well said:

"'Be pure, not by washing, but by thinking'"
("Jud. Bap.," p. 176).

A condition of mental purity is a baptism. Clement calls it "this baptism." A condition of ceremonial purity, a baptism by washing the hands, as done by Telemachus, is a symbol, "an image," of this baptism, which the heathen poets learned from Moses. This hand-washing baptism was a frequent practice, he says, among the Jews. The couch on which the Jews were accustomed thus to baptize was the dining couch, the triclinium on which they reclined at meals.

2. Theophylact, in his comment on Luke xi. 38, where Jesus reproves the Pharisee who "marvelled that he was not first baptized before dinner," says: "Jesus, deriding their foolish custom— I mean their purifying themselves before eating—

teaches that they ought to purify their souls by good works; for *washing the hands by water* purifies the body only, not the soul" (Beecher, p. 222; Dale, "Johannic Bap.," p. 117).

3. Origen: "The word of the precept, truly, with the feet, orders the washing with internal water, announcing figuratively the sacrament of baptism" ("Jud. Bap.," p. 175).

4. Cyril of Jerusalem: "The high-priest first washes, then sacrifices; for Aaron was first washed, then became high-priest. For how could he be permitted to pray for others who was not first cleansed by water? And the laver placed within the tent was a symbol of baptism" (p. 175).

The design of the water in the laver was for the cleansing of the high-priests. But they were not immersed in the laver; the water was *taken out* of the laver for use in their cleansing.

Dr. William Smith, in his "Dictionary of the Bible," edited by Professor H. B. Hackett, Vol. IV. p. 2877, says that "the water was drawn out by taps from the laver, so that the priests might be said to wash 'at,' not 'in,' it." Lightfoot, quoted on the same page, cites Jewish testimony making "twelve cocks (epistomia) for drawing off the water." The Septuagint translation of Exodus xxx. 19 teaches that the water was used for washing the hands and feet of the priests, not *in* the laver, but *out* of it. "Aaron and his sons shall wash their hands and feet with water *out of it.*" The water was taken "out" of the laver for the washing. The English version likewise says: "They shall wash their hands and feet *thereat.*" The Septuagint employs the word *nipto* to denote the washing of the priests in Ex. xxx. 19, a word that never means "dip." The Septuagint also employs the instrumental dative "with water." This is the more significant in contrast with the preposition *into* in the previous verse: "Pour water into it" (the laver). Cyril also uses the preposition *dia*, which denotes the means of cleansing—"cleansed *by* water." The water was not the element *into which* they were *dipped*, but the means *by which* they were *cleansed.*

CIRCUMCISION BAPTISM.

Circumcision and baptism both denote purification. The Patrists, therefore, call circumcision baptism.

1. Justin Martyr: "Wash you and be clean; and put away iniquities from your souls, as God commanded you to wash this washing and to circumcise the true circumcision. . . . What need, then, have I of circumcision, who have re-

ceived witness from God? What need is there of that baptism for me, who have been baptized by the Holy Spirit?" ("C. and P. B.," p. 540). Justin calls it "that baptism," yet in it there was neither dipping, nor pouring, nor sprinkling.

2. Chrysostom, Hom. xl: "There was pain and trouble in the practice of that Jewish circumcision; but our circumcision—I mean the grace of baptism—gives cure without pain, and this for infants as well as men" (Taylor's "Apostolic Baptism," p. 74).

3. Justin Martyr: "We Gentile Christians . . . have not received that circumcision which is according to the flesh, but that circumcision which is spiritual. . . . We have received this circumcision in baptism" ("Bib. Sacra," Vol. XV. p. 75).

4. Cyril: "We receive the spiritual seal, being circumcised through washing by the Holy Spirit. . . By the circumcision of Christ being buried with him by baptism" ("Jud. Bap.," p. 207).

5. Origen: "Christ came and gave to us the second circumcision by the baptism of regeneration, and purged our souls" (p. 207).

WATER BAPTIZED BY THE HOLY SPIRIT.

The Patrists did not believe that mere water in its natural state, in any mode of its use, could effect Christian baptism. They believed that the water must first be baptized —*i.e.*, purified—by the Holy Spirit, and, having thus received a divine, spiritual quality, it could effect Christian baptism in whatever mode applied. In this they deviated from the Bible teaching, which is that water-baptism is only a symbol of the baptism of the Holy Ghost. Yet the main idea which pervades all their writings, that baptism signifies purification, here applies in all its force.

1. Tertullian : " It is necessary, also, that the water be purified and sanctified first by the priest, that it may be able *by* ITS OWN *baptism* to cleanse the sins of the baptized man. For the Lord says, through the prophet Ezekiel, 'And I will sprinkle you with *pure* water, and I will purify you'" ("C. and P. B.," p. 541).

By being " purified and sanctified," the water is thoroughly *changed in its character*, and this purified condition is its " BAPTISM."

2. Ambrose : " Christ was therefore baptized, not that he might be sanctified by the waters, bu'

that he might *sanctify the waters*, and by his own purity purify the stream which he touches. . . . For when the Saviour is washed, the whole water is cleansed *for our baptism*" (p. 552).

3. Jerome: "How is the soul which has not the Holy Spirit purged from old defilements? For water does not wash the soul unless it is *first washed by the Holy Spirit, that it* MAY BE ABLE SPIRITUALLY *to wash others*" (p. 552).

4. Tertullian: "For neither can the Spirit operate without the water, nor the water without the Spirit" ("Jud. Bap.," p. 197).

The conjoint agency of both water and the Spirit is necessary.

5. Council of Carthage: "*For water only, unless it have the Holy Spirit also*, cannot purge sins or sanctify man. Wherefore they must admit the Holy Spirit to be there where they say baptism is, or that baptism is not where the Holy Spirit is not; *for baptism cannot be where the Holy Spirit is not*" ("C. and P. B.," p. 548).

Dipping can be without the Holy Spirit. But mere dipping is not Christian baptism in the judgment of the Patrists. Dipping a person in mere natural water is not Christian baptism. There can be no baptism with water unless the water itself is first baptized—*i.e.*, purified—by the Holy Spirit, that it may have a baptizing power.

6. Cyril of Jerusalem: "*Do not regard this washing as by* SIMPLE *water, but as by the spiritual grace given with the water.* . . . The *simple* water, receiving the invocation of the Holy Spirit, and of Christ, and of the Father, *acquires the* POWER *of sanctification*" (p. 554).

The Holy Spirit communicates a spiritual quality to the water, giving the water power to baptize. Mere water is insufficient.

7. Cyril of Alexandria: "We have not been baptized *by bare water,* . . . but by the Holy Spirit."

8. Justin Martyr: "Isaiah did not send you to the bath, there to wash away murder and other sins, which *not all the water of the sea* is sufficient to purify. . . . Be baptized as to the soul from anger, and avarice, and envy, and hate, and behold, the body is pure" (p. 598).

9. Jerome: "Do you offer to me THE SOUL *washed with* SIMPLE *water?* . . . The baptism of the Church without the Holy Spirit is nothing" ("C. and P. B.," p. 513).

10. Epiphanius: "Christ, baptized by John,

came to the waters, not needing washing, . . . *giving* THEM *power* for those who were to be perfected" (p. 552).

11. Cyril of Alexandria: "As water in a caldron, set to the fire, receives the force of the fire, so the water of baptism *by the Spirit* is raised to a divine and ineffable virtue" ("Johannic Baptism," p. 106).

12. Augustine: "The Holy Spirit works in that water, so that those who before baptism were guilty of many sins . . . merit, after baptism, the kingdom of heaven" (" C. and P. B.," p. 555).

Many other examples are given by Dr. Dale in his thorough discussion of this subject in " Patristic Baptism." He also traces to its source the error of uniting the Holy Spirit with the water in Christian baptism.

POURING BAPTISM.

1. Jerome: "And I will pour out [or sprinkle] upon you clean water. . . . I will pour out the clean water of saving baptism, and I will cleanse them" (" Jud. Bap.," p. 196).

2. Basil Magnus: "Elias has shown the power of baptism by burning the sacrifice upon the altar of burnt-offerings, not by means of fire, but by

means of water. . . . When the water is mystically poured thrice upon the altar, the fire begins and kindles into a flame, as though it were oil" ("C. and P. B.," p. 536).

3. Origen, on 1 Kings xviii. 34, where Elijah commanded water to be poured three times upon the sacrifice on the altar, says: "But why is it believed that the coming Elias will baptize, when he did not baptize what needed cleansing upon the wood of the altar? . . . For he commanded the priests to effect this baptism" ("C. and P. B.," p. 535).

The baptism was a *cleansing* (loutron) effected by pouring water. The baptism did not consist in the act of pouring, but in the *effect* of the water which they poured. Baptism does not consist in the act, but in the effect of the baptizing agency.

4. Gregory Nazianzen: "I have three overflowings with which I will purify the sacrifice, kindling fire by water" (p. 536).

5. Ambrose: "Baptism, like a fire, consumes sins, for Christ baptizes by fire and the Spirit. You read this type in the Books of the Kings (1 Kings xviii. 34), where Elias put wood upon the altar, and said that they should throw over it water from water-pots. . . . Thou, O man!

art upon the altar, who shalt be cleansed by water" (p. 537.)

6. Jerome: "And I will no more pour out upon them the waters of saving baptism, but the waters of doctrine and of the Word of God" (p. 534).

7. Ambrose, on 2 Maccabees i. 20–36, "Nehemiah commanded the water that was left to be poured upon the great stones. When this was done there was kindled a flame. . . . It was told the King of Persia that Nehemiah had purified the sacrifices therewith," says: "The narrative of the preceding event . . . betokens the Holy Spirit and Christian baptism" (p. 538).

8. Bernard, speaking of the baptism of our Saviour by John, says: "The creature pours water on the head of the Creator" (Fairchild, p. 63, note).

SPRINKLING BAPTISM.

1. Cyril of Jerusalem: "Thou seest the power of baptism. Be of good courage, O Jerusalem! The Lord will take away all thine iniquities. . . . He will sprinkle upon you clean water, and ye shall be purified from all your sin" ("Jud. Bap.," p. 196).

2. Didymus Alexandrinus: "The very image of baptism both continually illuminated and saved all Israel at that time, . . . as prophesied Ezekiel, xxxvi. 25: 'I will sprinkle clean water upon you, and you shall be clean from all your sins'; and David, Psalm l. 9: 'Sprinkle me with hyssop, and I shall be clean'" (p. 196).

3. Jerome, in his interpretation of Ez. xxxvi. 25, thus expresses it: "I will pour out or sprinkle upon you clean water," using both words, *effundam sive aspergam*, showing that the baptism does not consist in the act, which is a matter of indifference, but in the effect." He says: "It is to be observed that a new heart and a new spirit may be given *by the pouring and sprinkling of water*" (p. 196).

He thus gives emphasis to the validity of pouring and sprinkling as modes of applying the baptismal agency. The baptism is a change in the spiritual condition of the soul effected by the pouring or sprinkling of water. He does not mean that *mere water* can save, for he says in another place: "Baptism is not without the Holy Spirit" ("C. and P. B." p. 552).

4. Petilianus: "Blush, O persecutors! ye make martyrs like unto Christ, whom [quos], after the

water of true baptism, baptizing blood sprinkles" ("C. and P. B.," p. 40).

It is the quality of the baptizing agency which effects the baptism, not the mode of its application. It can be applied by sprinkling.

5. Ambrose, on 2 Mac. i. 20-36, where we read, "When the sacrifices were laid on, Nehemiah commanded the priests to sprinkle with the water both the wood and that which lay upon it. When this was done . . . there was a great fire kindled, . . . the sacrifice was consumed"— commenting on this, Ambrose says: "The narrative of the preceding event, and especially of the sacrifice offered by Nehemiah, betokens the Holy Spirit and the baptism of Christians" (p. 538: "Jud. Bap.," p. 346).

6. Tertullian, speaking of heathen nations, says: "They everywhere purify villas, houses, temples, and whole cities by sprinkling water. . . . Here we see the work of the devil emulating the things of God, since he practises even baptism among his own people" ("C. and P. B." p. 532).

7. Ambrose, on clinic baptism, which was performed by sprinkling, says: "There are not wanting sick persons who are baptized, almost daily" (p. 532).

8. Basil Magnus, speaking of the baptism of Ariantheus, who was baptized by his wife by sprinkling on his death-bed, calls it a purification: "He washed away all the stains of his soul at the close of his life by the washing [loutron] of regeneration" (p. 501).

9. The Codex Sinaiticus has the word "sprinkled" instead of "baptized" in Mark vii. 4. It reads: "Except they sprinkle themselves from the market," instead of "Except they baptize themselves" (Tischendorf, New Testament, Leipsic, 1873). In accounting for the variation, it must be admitted that the copyist "saw no difficulty in a baptism being effected by sprinkling."

10. Lactantius: "So, also, he would save the Gentiles by baptism—that is, *by the sprinkling of the purifying dew*" ("Johannic Baptism," p. 317).

11. Cyprian quotes the following passages from the Old Testament to prove that baptism by sprinkling was equally valid with other modes: "The Holy Scripture says, Ez. xxxvi. 25, 26: 'I will sprinkle clean water upon you, and ye shall be cleansed from all your uncleanness, and from all your idols will I cleanse you; and I will give a new heart to you, and put a new spirit within you'; likewise in Num. xix. 8, 12, 13: . . . 'He

shall not be clean, and that soul shall be cut off from Israel, because the water of sprinkling was not sprinkled upon him'; and again, Num. viii. 5, 7: 'The Lord spake to Moses, saying: . . . Thus shalt thou purify them : Thou shalt sprinkle them with the water of purification'; and again, Num. xix. 9: 'The water of sprinkling is purification.' *Whence it appears that the sprinkling of water* POSSESSES EQUAL VALUE *with the saving washing*" ("C. and P. B.," p. 524).

CHAPTER III.

SPECIAL DISCUSSION OF SIRACH XXXIV. 30.

THE view given above is that the purification which Sirach calls a baptism is effected wholly by the agency of heifer-ashes.

To this view an objection has been drawn from Num. xix. 19: "And the clean person shall sprinkle upon the unclean on the third day, and on the seventh day: and on the seventh day he shall purify himself, and wash his clothes, and bathe himself in water, and shall be clean at even." The objection is that the purification consists either wholly, or chiefly, or in part in washing the clothes and bathing in water.

But this verse alone in itself is not decisive. Viewed in itself alone, it admits of more than one interpretation, and it has received a diversity of interpretations. When the meaning of a passage is ambiguous and doubtful, the rule of interpretation is to resort to the context and other sources for aid in ascertaining its true meaning. That this necessity exists in Num. xix. 19 is evident rom the diversity of interpretation to which it has given rise.

1. Dr. Fairbairn ("Hermeneutical Manual," p. 298) explains the baptism of Sirach as referring to the "purification for those who had come into contact with a corpse; and this, we learn from Num. xix. 13, 19, included a threefold action—sprinkling the person with water mixed with the ashes of a red heifer, bathing it, and washing the clothes. Plainly, therefore, the baptism of the son of Sirach is a general term expressive of the whole of these, . . . all the ablutions practised on the occasion."

This makes the baptism a purification; but it makes the process a complex operation, "a threefold action," to which no allusion is elsewhere ever made.

2. Dr. Gale makes the baptism consist chiefly in washing the clothes and bathing: "A further washing is necessary besides the sprinklings, . . . and this washing was the finishing of the ceremony. The defiled person was to be sprinkled with the holy water on the third and on the seventh day, only as a preparatory to the great purification, which was to be by washing the body and clothes on the seventh day."

This interpretation Dr. Fairbairn rejects, because it makes the "bathing at the close the chief thing," while it "was evidently one of the least."

The fatal objection is that it makes that "the great purification" which is never spoken of elsewhere as any part of the purification; and it makes that "only a preparatory to the great purification" which is elsewhere the only thing spoken of as the purification.

3. Dr. Carson wholly excludes the agency of the heifer-ashes from the baptism, and makes it consist in "immersion only." It is "his *dipping* or *baptism*" (pp. 66, 320, 455).

4. Dr. Geo. D. Armstrong ("The Doctrine of Baptisms," p. 72) says that the person who in Num. xix. 19 was required to "wash his clothes and bathe himself in water," was not the person upon whom the ashes were sprinkled, but it was the person who did the sprinkling. Dr. Armstrong thinks the pronoun "he" in the expression, "he shall purify himself," has for its antecedent "the clean person," and that this person sprinkled the ashes, and then washed his own clothes and bathed himself, and that the man who was defiled by a dead body was only required to have the heifer-ashes sprinkled upon him.

But if there be an uncertainty in the verse

itself respecting the antecedent of the pronoun, the context is decisive against making the clean person the antecedent. The clean person, after sprinkling the ashes, was only required to "wash his clothes" (v. 21), but the other was required to "wash his clothes and bathe himself in water" (v. 19).

This interpretation also leaves unsolved the query why all the others who came in contact with the heifer-ashes should be required to wash their clothes, and some of them also to bathe, while the man on whom the ashes were sprinkled was alone exempt from this requirement. Would not the contact with the heifer-ashes render the use of water as needful for him as for them?

5. The interpretation of Dr. Dale is that there were two different kinds of defilement, from two different and opposite sources: one from touching a dead body, the other from touching the heifer-ashes; and that these two different kinds of defilement were removed respectively by two different agencies. The defilement from a dead body was removed by heifer-ashes, the defilement from the heifer-ashes was removed by water; and as the person whose purification is described in Numbers xix. 19 had incurred both kinds of defilement, he needed both kinds of puri-

fication. From the defilement he had contracted by touching a dead body he was purified by the heifer-ashes sprinkled upon him. But while the ashes had power to remove from him the defilement from the touch of a dead body, they imparted to him another sort of defilement, as they did to all the others with whom they came in contact; and this defilement was removed by the agency of water.

This is the only interpretation which is consistent in all respects with the context, and with all the facts and testimonies that relate to the subject.

1. There are two kinds of ceremonial defilement mentioned in this chapter, arising from two different and opposite sources. One kind of defilement resulted from touching a dead body. "He that toucheth the dead body of any man shall be unclean seven days" (v. 11). The other kind of defilement was incidental, resulting from contact with the heifer-ashes, the water of separation. "He that toucheth the water of separation shall be unclean until even" (v. 21).

2. These different kinds of defilement were removed by different agencies: the one by heifer-ashes, the other by water. The defilement from a dead body was the greater; and for the removal

Special Discussion of Sirach xxxiv. 30. 77

of this greater defilement the elaborate preparation of the heifer-ashes was required. The lighter and incidental defilement caused by the heifer-ashes was removed by the use of water. The examples described by Moses in this chapter make this sufficiently plain. These persons had not touched a dead body, but, in preparing the heifer-ashes and applying them, they contracted a defilement, and were required to make use of water for purification.

"The priest shall wash his clothes, and he shall bathe his flesh in water, and . . . shall be unclean until the even" (v. 7).

"And he that burneth" the heifer "shall wash his clothes in water, and bathe his flesh in water, and shall be unclean until the even" (v. 8). "And he that gathereth the ashes of the heifer shall wash his clothes, and be unclean until the even" (v. 10).

Also, "he that sprinkleth the water of separation shall wash his clothes" (v. 21). He was clean before he sprinkled the water of separation, but he incurred defilement in the act of sprinkling the ashes.

As all the other persons incurred defilement by contact with the heifer-ashes, so the man on whom the ashes were sprinkled incurred the same kind of defilement; and as they were required to make use of water for its removal, he also was required to do the same. "On the seventh day he shall purify himself, and wash his clothes, and bathe himself in water, and shall be clean at even" (v. 19). He had incurred a double defilement, and therefore was required to have a double purification.

The defilement from touching a dead body was a much deeper defilement, requiring a more effective agency for its removal. A blood-red heifer must be slain and burnt, and her ashes must be mixed with water, and this consecrated mixture must be applied on the third day and on the seventh day.

3. The purification from the defilement by a dead body was accomplished *solely by the agency of heifer-ashes*.

It was for this purpose that the ashes were prepared and kept. The ashes of the heifer "shall be kept for the congregation of the children of Israel for a water of separation: it is a purification for sin" (v. 9). "For an unclean person they shall take of the ashes of the burnt heifer of purification for sin" (v. 17).

It was by means of the ashes that the person defiled was purified and made clean. "He that toucheth the dead body of any man shall be unclean seven days. He shall purify himself with it on the third day, and on the seventh day he shall be clean " (vs. 11, 12).

The sprinkling of the ashes was the only thing for the neglect of which the penalty for non-compliance with the requirement was inflicted. " Whosoever toucheth the dead body of any man that is dead, and purifieth not himself, . . . that soul shall be cut off from Israel: because the water of separation was not sprinkled upon him " (v. 13).

This is made doubly prominent by the emphatic repetition of the penalty for neglect of the sprinkling. " That soul shall be cut off from among the congregation, because he hath defiled the sanctuary of the Lord : the water of separation hath not been sprinkled upon him: he is unclean " (v. 20). Thus with emphasis it is made to appear that the sole agency of the heifer-ashes is the *one essential thing* in this purification.

4. The two classes of cases are entirely distinct from each other. The points of difference are numerous and broad.

1. The sources of defilement were different: the one from touching a dead body, the other from contact with the heifer-ashes.

2. The duration of the two kinds of defilement was different: the one lasting seven days, the other only one day.

3. The means of purification were different: the one heifer-ashes, the other water.

4. The modes of applying the different agencies were different: the one by sprinkling, the other by washing the clothes and bathing in water.

5. The number of times in which the agencies must be applied were different: in the one case twice, in the other only once.

6. The persons performing the operation were different: in the one case another person must apply the purifying agency; in the other the person himself must do it by his own act.

7. In the one case the agency was heifer-ashes only; in the other, water only.

Thus clear, broad, and distinct are the two classes of cases. The failure to distinguish between them has been a fruitful source of obscurity and error.

The distinction of the two classes which Moses makes in the context of Num. xix. 19 determines the true interpretation of that verse. It makes it clear that the interpretation of Dr. Dale is the true one. The sole agency for the removal of the defilement from a dead body was the

Special Discussion of Sirach xxxiv. 30. 81

sprinkling of the heifer-ashes. The use of water was for the removal of another and different defilement.

This interpretation is confirmed by the unanimous testimony of Jewish, inspired, and Patristic writers.

1. The great Jewish historian Josephus, in his description of this purification, represents it as accomplished solely by the sprinkling of heifer-ashes. In his "Antiquities of the Jews," IV. iv. 6, he has informed us what the process of this purification was. He says: "Moses purified the people after this manner"; and, having given the description, he adds: "When this purification, . . . as it has now been described, was over." I will give Dr. Conant's translation of the text of Immanuel Bekker (ed. 1868, p. 33):

"Those, therefore, who were defiled by the dead body, casting a little of the ashes into a fountain and dipping a hyssop branch, they sprinkled on the third and seventh of the days."

Thus, even according to the reading of Immanuel Bekker, and the translation by T. J. Conant, *the one and only* thing which was done for the purification of those defiled by the dead body was sprinkling upon them the ashes prepared for this purpose; and this is what Sirach calls a baptism.

2. Philo, another Jewish writer, nearly contemporary with Josephus, and, like him, well versed in the knowledge of Jewish customs, gives his testimony, in harmony with that of Josephus, to the nature of this Jewish rite. He says: "Moses does this philosophically; for most others are sprinkled with unmixed water, some with sea or river water, others with water drawn from the fountains. But Moses employed ashes for this purpose. Then, as to the manner, they put them into a vessel, pour on water, then moisten branches of hyssop with the mixture, then sprinkle it upon those who are to be purified" ("Jud. Bap.," p. 101).

3. A greater than Josephus and Philo, the Apostle Paul, has described this rite (Heb. ix. 13), and he teaches that the purification was accomplished by the sprinkling of heifer-ashes. "The ashes of a heifer sprinkling the unclean sanctifieth to the purifying of the flesh."

4. Cyril of Alexandria, on Isa. iv. 4, says: "We have not been baptized by bare water, nor yet by the ashes of a heifer, (since we have been sprinkled for the purification of the flesh only, according to the saying of the blessed Paul), but by the Holy Spirit."

5. The same writer, on Isa. i. 16, speaking of 'the water of purifying" as a type of baptism, says: "What the water of purifying is the most wise Paul shall teach, saying, The ashes of a heifer sprinkling the unclean."

6. Gregory Nazianzen: "Therefore let us be baptized, that we may overcome; let us partake of the purifying waters . . . more sanctifying than the ashes of a heifer sprinkling the unclean, and having, for the time, power for the purification of the body."

There is complete unanimity in the testimony, extending over the interval of five hundred years from Sirach to Cyril, that the purification from defilement by a dead body was accomplished by the sole agency of the sprinkling of heifer-ashes. This Sirach, Cyril, and others call a baptism.

Another point in this special discussion which requires attention is the translation of the last word in Sirach xxxiv. 30 (loutron). Dale translates: "What is he benefited by his *cleansing?*" Carson: "What availeth his *dipping?*"

The translation of Dr. Carson is shown to be erroneous by the unanimous testimony of Josephus and all the other Greek writers who refer to this subject. They all with one voice describe this rite as a purification effected by the sprinkling of heifer-ashes. The appeal to Num. xi. 19, isolated from its connection with the context, proves nothing, on account of the ambiguity of the passage. Elsewhere all the facts and all the testimonies are clear and decisive that the baptism was a purification effected by the sprinkling of the heifer-ashes.

The translation "cleansing," which Dr. Dale gives, is sustained also by the most ample proof from the usage of the Greek word.

1. Even in classical Greek it sometimes denotes "offerings for purification." Hermann Cremer, "Bib. Theo. Lex.," p. 418, refers to passages in proof of this signification.

2. In Hellenistic Greek this is its usual signification, as Dale has shown in "Christic and Patristic Baptism." A few examples are here selected. Basil, speaking of the baptism of the prætor Ariantheus, who was baptized by his wife by sprinkling on his dying-bed, says: "He washed away all the stains of his soul at the close of his life by the *washing* [loutron] of regeneration" (p. 501).

This example is decisive. The "washing" was not a dipping, but a purification by sprinkling, a cleansing.

Justin Martyr: "Therefore through the *wash-*

Special Discussion of Sirach xxxiv. 30. 85

ing [loutron] of repentance . . . is the only baptism which is able to cleanse the repenting" (p. 501). The word here means spiritual washing, a *cleansing*, as Justin explains it.

The same writer says: "And the demons, having heard of this *washing* [loutron], . . . required their worshippers to sprinkle themselves" (p. 501).

Origen says: "That which was upon the wood of the altar needed *cleansing* [loutron]" ("Jud. Bap.," p. 328). This cleansing was effected by pouring on water.

Clemens Alexandrinus: "It is called *washing* [loutron] because we are cleansed from our sins" ("C. and P. B.," p. 553).

The same writer: "It is especially necessary to wash the soul by the purifying word. . . . Therefore the best *washing* [loutron] cleanses the defilement of the soul, and is spiritual" (p. 506).

3. In New Testament Greek the word always means purification, *cleansing*. Prof. Stuart translates and explains Tit. iii. 5: "*He saved us by* THE WASHING [loutron] *of regeneration—i.e.*, by that purification or cleansing which regeneration confers." In Eph. v. 26 he also translates it *washing*, and explains it to mean "cleansing" ("Bib. Rep." iii. 336).

4. The lexicons give the word the same signification. Robinson, in his "Lexicon of the New Testament," after giving its classical meanings—*bath, water for bathing, washing*—gives as its meaning in the New Testament *a washing, ablution*.

Hermann Cremer, in his "Biblico-Theological Lexicon of New Testament Greek," applies the word "purification" as the signification of this word in Eph. v. 26, Tit. iii. 5, and Sirach xxxiv. 30.

BATHING.

Dr. Conant, BAPTIZEIN, 1868, p. 86, translates the last part of Sirach xxxiv. 30: "What is he profited by his bathing?" meaning by bathing *immersion*. The word bathing is used in Num. xix. 19, "Shall bathe himself in water," and it is claimed that bathing is done by immersion. The Greek word *louo* is used in Num. xix. 19 and elsewhere in the Old Testament (Sept.), and from this verb the noun *loutron*, which is used in Sirach xxxiv. 30, is derived. The subject has been much discussed. The examples quoted above, and others in Dale, prove that in its religious use, both ritual and spiritual, the word signifies purification. The whole argument for immersion rests on the fact that bathing was sometimes performed by immersion, *overlooking* the fact that it was also performed in other and various modes, and not taking cognizance of its religious usage in the sense of purification. I will append some testimonies concerning other modes of bathing.

Bathing was frequently performed in Oriental countries *by pouring* and other modes.

In Dr. William Smith's " Dictionary of Christian Antiquities," 1875, Vol. I. p. 168, it is stated that " one common mode of bathing among the ancients was the pouring of water from vessels over the body. . . . And it is remarkable that, in almost all the earliest representations of baptism that have been preserved to us, this is the special act represented."

In Smith's "Dictionary of Greek and Roman Antiquities," third American edition, by Charles Anthon, LL.D., under the article *Loutron*, p. 598, Dr. Smith says: "On ancient vases, on which persons are represented bathing, we never find anything corresponding to a modern bath, in which persons can stand or sit; but there is always a round or oval basin (λουτήρ or λουτήριον) resting on a stand, by the side of which those who are bathing are represented standing undressed and washing themselves, as is seen in the following woodcut, taken from Sir W. Hamilton's vases.

The word *demosia* upon it shows that it belonged to a public bath."

Dr. Smith, "Dic. of Gr. and Rom. Ant.," p. 143, speaks of the vessel for bathing which, in the age of Homer, was called *asaminthos*, and says: "It would appear, from the description of the bath administered to Ulysses in the palace of Circe, that this vessel *did not contain water itself*, but was only used for the bather to sit in while the warm water *was poured over him*, which was heated in a large caldron or tripod, under which the fire was placed, and, when sufficiently warmed, was taken out in other vessels and *poured over the head and shoulders* of the person who sat in the asaminthos. . . . The vessel was of polished marble, like the basins (labra) which have been discovered in the Roman baths." There were "similar basins," says Prof. Wilson, "at the porticos of Christian churches, in the earlier centuries, for washing the hands."

Among the paintings in an ancient tomb at Thebes, described by Sir Gardner Wilkinson in his work on "The Manners and Customs of the Ancient Egyptians," is one which contains a representation of a lady enjoying the luxury of a bath: "One attendant removes the jewelry and clothes she has taken off, or suspends them to a stand in the apartment; another *pours water from a vase over her head*, as the third rubs her arms and body with her open hands; and a fourth, seated near her, holds a sweet-scented flower to her nose, and supports her as she sits (on a carpet or mat)." Wilkinson further says: "The same subject is treated nearly in the same manner on some of the Greek vases, *the water being poured over the bather*, who kneels or is seated on the ground. The mode of bathing in Egypt is thus identified with that of Greece" ("Jud. Bap.," p. 121).

Rev. Mr. Löwenthal, missionary in India, says: "The Hindoos use a small urn, called *lota*, with which they bathe at the river, *pouring water over the body*" (p. 122).

In Ovid's description of Diana's bath, he says: "They *pour water out* of the urns" (urnis undam effundunt).

Porphyry says: "It was customary for married women to purify maidens by sprinkling or affusion, before marriages, with water taken from fountains and living springs." Photius tells us "that the water used for this purpose was brought in a pitcher" ("C. and P. B.," p. 501). The water was sometimes brought by a boy, and sometimes by a girl, as the representations on ancient monuments indicate ("Dic. of Gr. and Rom. Ant.," p. 599).

Dr. Dale says: "The common way of bathing among the Greeks was not by immersion, but by pouring water over the body" ("C. and P. B.," p. 504). Prof. Stuart says of the word as used in the Old Testament: "Neither *washing* nor *bathing* appears to be the same as plunging or immersing; for neither the word *tabal, to immerse*, nor the word *shataph, to inundate*, is used in reference to these ceremonial washings" (p. 340). "We find no example among all the Levitical washings or ablutions where immersion of the person is required. The word *rahats*, which is almost uniformly employed, and which our translators have rendered *wash* and *bathe*, does not imply *immersion*" (p. 341). Even Dr. Carson, near the close of his discussion, says of louo: "That the word does not necessarily express mode, I readily admit" (p. 486). All the historic facts that relate to the usage of the word in its different forms furnish demonstration that it does not denote a definite and specific act, *to dip*, but is used in the general sense of washing, or cleansing by any of the different modes of applying the cleansing agency. The effort to force the word in Sirach xxxiv. 30 to signify *a dipping* is without warrant in the usage of the word, and is in complete opposition to the universal testimony of ancient writers, Moses, Josephus, Philo, Paul, Cyril, and the rest, that the loutron which Sirach calls a baptism is a cleansing by sprinkling the heifer-ashes on the person needing purification.

CHAPTER IV.

GENUINENESS OF THE QUOTATION FROM JOSEPHUS.

THERE is one phrase in the quotation from Josephus which is omitted in the text of Immanuel Bekker. Dr. Dale refers to this omission in his "Judaic Baptism," but gives good reasons for retaining the common reading as given in the other critical editions and in the manuscripts of the works of Josephus. As the value of the quotation in relation to baptism depends on the genuineness of the words omitted by Bekker, I will give the reasons in proof of their genuineness. I am indebted to Dr. Dale for the means of proof, not only as given in his book, but for the Greek and Latin quotations from critical editions of Josephus. That the words omitted by Bekker are genuine is proved by the fact that no good reason has ever been given for their omission, and that they are found in the manuscripts and in all the critical editions of the works of Josephus, except that of Bekker.

1. The reading of the passage given by Dr.

Dale is *the common reading*. This is acknowledged by Dr. Conant, who calls it "the common Greek text," "the common reading," and he gives it (BAPTIZEIN, 1868, p. 33) in a note precisely as it is given by Dr. Dale.

2. William Whiston, in his translation of Josephus, 1737, gives the whole passage, without the slightest intimation of a different reading. Elsewhere he notices the various readings in the copious notes to his translation, but makes no allusion to any variation in this passage. He had ample means of knowing, for in a note, "Ant.," xviii. iv. 6, he says of a certain date that it is made out by "a calculation from *all Josephus' Greek copies.*" He had before him, also, Hudson's critical edition, to which he frequently refers as of the highest authority, and he doubtless was satisfied with the judgment of Hudson, who rejects Bekker's alteration and retains the common reading.

3. Hudson, Principal of St. Mary's Hall, Oxford, in his critical edition of the works of Josephus, bearing date 1720, gives the reading of this passage just as it is given by Dr. Dale. This edition was the work of an eminent scholar, critically prosecuted, with voluminous and learned notes. On the title-page of his edition we read:

"FLAVII JOSEPHI
OPERA OMNIA.
OXONII,
MDCCXX.

Ad codices fere omnes cum impressos tum manuscriptos diligenter recensuit, nova versione donavit, et notis illustravit Joannes Hudsonus, S.T.P., Aulæ Beatæ Mariæ Virginis Principalis, et Protobibliothecarius Bodleianus."

The text of Hudson's edition, it thus appears, is the result of a careful collation of "almost all the printed editions and manuscript copies" of the works of Josephus to be found. Thus his edition conforms to the printed editions and manuscript copies previously existing.

Immanuel Bekker, taking up a suggestion which had been thrown out by Bonfrère, erased the phrase in question in his edition. The reading of Bekker, translated by Conant, was given chap. iii. p. 81. Hudson had Bonfrère's suggestion before him, thoughtfully considered it, found it wanting in validity, *and rejected it.*

4. Nearly two centuries earlier, in 1544, the critical edition of Jerome Frobenus and Nicholas Episcopius was printed at Basle, in Switzerland. This edition was printed within the first century after the discovery of printing. There must

have been copies of the manuscript of Josephus, if not printed editions, which contained the passage as it stands in this edition, and which came down from earlier periods and centuries. On the title-page we read:

"FLAVII JOSEPHI OPERA,
HIERONYMUS FROBENUS ET NICOLAUS EPISCOPIUS.
BASILEÆ, MDXLIIII."

The Greek text of the passage of Josephus under consideration is given in this edition as follows. A single sentence from the preceding period is for a special reason prefixed:

Ξύλον κέδρινον εἰς μέσον ἐμβάλλουσι τὸ πῦρ, καὶ ὕσσωπον, καὶ φοινικτὸν ἔριον. . . . Τοὺς οὖν ἀπὸ νεκροῦ μεμιασμένους, τῆς τέφρας ὀλίγον εἰς πηγὴν ἐνιέντες καὶ ὕσσωπον, βαπτίσαντες τε καὶ τῆς τέφρας ταυτῆς εἰς πηγὴν, ἐρραινον τρίτῃ καὶ ἑβδόμῃ τῶν ἡμερῶν· καὶ καθαροὶ τὸ λοιπὸν ἦσαν. Τοῦτο δὲ καὶ κατελθοῦσι εἰς τὰς κληρουχίας προσέταξε ποιεῖν.

The entire text as given above is the same, without the change of a single word, in both Hudson's edition of 1720 and the Basle edition of 1544. The sole difference is that the comma after "πηγὴν" is the punctuation of Hudson; there is no mark of punctuation after this word in the "Basileæ" edition. The Greek colon after "ἡμερῶν" is also that of Hudson; the punctuating mark in the "Basileæ" is a comma. The difference is very minute, and has no effect upon the meaning.

5. And now what reason is given for omitting a part of this text? It is found in all the manuscripts and in all the printed editions of Josephus, except that of Bekker. The *erasure* of words from an ancient writer cannot be justified by any light reason. Jacques Bonfrère, a Jesuit, in his Latin "Commentary on the Pentateuch," A.D. 1625, failing to interpret Num. xix. 19 so as to elicit a meaning that seemed to harmonize with the common reading of the passage in Josephus, suggested the omission of the phrase τε καὶ τῆς τέφρας ταύτης εἰς πηγήν. Two hundred years later Immanuel Bekker, in his edition of Josephus, too hastily adopted the suggestion of Bonfrère. Instead of such mutilation of an ancient author, the more scholarly method would have been to seek a better understanding of the real meaning of both Moses and Josephus. But, we ask, what is the reason given for this erasure? "Some words," it is said, "are repeated." The common text reads: "Putting a little of the ashes and a hyssop-branch into a spring, and baptizing of this ashes [put] into the spring."

The reason given is not a good one. There is

no repetition in the thought. The clause in which the words "ashes" and "into the spring" are repeated, expresses *an additional thought*, and this additional thought is *essential* to the description of the process of purification. Josephus first tells us how the ashes were prepared for use, and then he tells us how they were used. First they prepare the ashes for use by mixing them with spring-water. When thus prepared, they make use of them for purifying the persons defiled. There was a good and sufficient reason for the repetition of the words, and Josephus employs the expression of design. Only four Greek words are repeated, and between them is a new word which shows that Josephus had a reason for using this expression. Common ashes would not be suitable for the work of purification. Therefore Josephus says: "They sprinkle the defiled with *this* ashes"—*i.e.*, the ashes which had been mixed with the spring-water. Thus, when we look beyond the mere words to the thought, and perceive the facts of the narration, the objection wholly disappears. Such a shallow reason as this for the erasure of words from the works of an ancient author cannot find acceptance with considerate scholars. It would make havoc with ancient and modern writings. In the very next chapter of Josephus, the expression, "the Hebrews," occurs four times in one sentence. If words are to be struck out for such a reason, authors would be mutilated without mercy at the arbitrary will of any one who either does not understand a passage, or who wishes to get rid of words which he does not like to accept.

6. There are other internal reasons in the Greek of Josephus which scholars give for rejecting the change in the common reading which Bonfrère proposes, and for rejecting the punctuation introduced to sustain it. One reason is found in the change which it makes in the style of Josephus as shown in the immediately preceding passage: "They cast cedar wood into the midst of the fire, and hyssop and scarlet wool." Here, in the Greek sentence (the Greek idiom being unlike the English, as Greek scholars will perceive), one accusative precedes and another follows the Greek verb. The same Greek idiom appears, as we should naturally expect, in the succeeding passage (although it cannot be shown in the translation): "Introducing a little of the ashes into the spring [water], and hyssop." But Bonfrère breaks up this harmony by his erasure and by connecting "hyssop" with "$\beta\alpha\pi\tau\iota\sigma\alpha\nu\tau\epsilon\varsigma$." Other reasons in the Greek style of Josephus

are given, but it is not needful here to discuss them.

7. Hudson found in one edition or manuscript which he examined a preposition supplied by the editor or copyist, which shows that that editor did not accept the judgment of Bonfrère. Hudson says: "Est qui legit βαπτίσαντες μετὰ δὲ τῆς τέφρας," etc. This editor or copyist, by inserting this Greek preposition, indicates that he regarded the ashes to be under the control of βαπτίσαντες, "baptizing *with* this ashes." But there is no need of a preposition to convey the meaning of Josephus. In conformity with a common rule of Greek grammar, he employs the genitive case without the preposition to denote the material by means of which the purification was effected. "The origin, source, and material are put in the genitive" (Crosby, Greek Grammar, sec. 412). The ashes are the *material* for accomplishing the purification. The translation of Dale gives the true meaning: "Baptizing *by* this ashes, . . . they sprinkle on the third and seventh day" (p. 387).

WILLIAM WHISTON'S TRANSLATION OF JOSEPHUS.

" When, therefore, any persons were defiled by a dead body, they put a little of these ashes into spring-water with hyssop, and, dipping part of these ashes in it, they sprinkled them with it, both on the third day and on the seventh, and after that they were clean. This he enjoined them to do also when the tribes should come into their own land." This version is not quoted by genuine scholars in the baptismal controversy; but as it has been quoted against Dale, and is liable to be quoted so again by those who have only a superficial knowledge of the subject, the following reasons for rejecting it are here republished from " The Reviewer Reviewed."

1. The ashes, even in Whiston's translation, were already put into the spring, mixing with water, and therefore ready for use, *before* he came to what he calls " dipping part of these ashes in it." Why, then, does he speak of dipping part of these ashes in it when they were *already in?*

2. The word "part" in the phrase "dipping part of these ashes" is not in the original. It is an interpolation made by the translator without the knowledge or consent of Josephus.

3. The idea of "dipping ashes" is absurd. Moses speaks of dipping the hyssop-branch into the water of separation preparatory to sprinkling the defiled ; but the idea of "dipping ashes" is

one for which neither Moses nor Josephus is responsible.

4. Hard pressed by this absurdity, Dr. Carson (p. 289) says: "The ashes must have been put into the water in a bag, as in cookery." And how much better does this make it? The whole idea of dipping ashes, and doing it by putting them into a bag, is a fiction invented to prop a modern theory which conflicts with the description given of this rite in the original language of Josephus.

A translation encumbered by such difficulties I reject, and adopt the translation of Dale, which is true to every word of the Greek, and gives a meaning free from absurdity. . . .

As Whiston was mistaken in his philosophy when he maintained that the deluge of Noah was caused by the tail of a comet, and as he was mistaken in his interpretation of prophecy when he predicted that the millennium would commence in 1766 ("New Am. Cyc.," XVI. 394), so, in his translation of this passage, he has been untrue to the Greek of Josephus, and misled the mere English reader by a translation which is absurd.

The quotation from Josephus is genuine, and is rightly translated by Dr. Dale. It gives a twofold testimony to the current use of the Greek word baptizo among the Jewish people to denote ceremonial purification by the sprinkling of heifer-ashes. The complete description which it gives, even in the reading of Immanuel Bekker, of the purification which Sirach calls a baptism, furnishes absolute demonstration that this baptism is effected by the sole agency of the heifer-ashes. It also gives the direct testimony of Josephus to the same truth; for the whole passage is genuine, according to the universal testimony of the manuscripts of Josephus, and all the critical editions of Josephus, except that of Bekker; and the reason which Bekker gives for the *erasure* is so unsubstantial that it is rejected by the most competent and impartial scholars, like Hudson, as wholly invalid, and the original and common reading is retained.

CHAPTER V.

BAPTISMS IN THE SEPTUAGINT.

IN the third century before Christ the Hebrew Scriptures were translated into the Greek language, and in this Greek Version the Apocryphal books of the Old Testament were incorporated. It is called the Septuagint because its translation was attributed to seventy Jewish elders. It is written in Hellenistic Greek, or, as it is sometimes called, Jewish Greek, and is the oldest monument of that kind of Greek extant. "The basis of the Hellenistic language of the New Testament," says Alexander Buttmann, "is the so-called Macedo-Alexandrian dialect, which became current in the time of the Ptolemies, especially at Alexandria, then the seat of culture." This became the vernacular language of the Greek-speaking Jews after they lost the popular use of the Hebrew in the time of the Babylonish captivity, and after the conquest of Alexander the Great had brought them under Grecian sway. The peculiarities of Hellenistic Greek as spoken by the Jews arose from the expression of Hebrew ideas and Hebrew modes of thought in the Greek language. This gave a Hebrew coloring and a Hebrew signification to a multitude of Greek words. This Hellenic dialect was known and spoken throughout the Roman Empire by the Hellenistic Jews who adopted the Greek civilization.

As the New Testament was written in Hellenistic and not in classic Greek, and as a large number of classic Greek words underwent an essential modification in their use by the Jews and the Christian fathers, who received the Scriptures from the Jews, the special usage of words like baptizo in Hellenistic Greek requires especial attention. It has been a great error to look exclusively to the classic usage of this word, and almost wholly overlook its Hellenistic usage. By fastening the attention on one single meaning of the word in its primary classic use, and by failing to give due consideration to those numerous passages which, with equal clearness, teach a secondary use, the truth is kept out of sight.

The historic origin of the signification *to purify* in the Greek word baptizo is found in the employment of this word by the Jews to express the purificatory rites enjoined in the Hebrew Scriptures. The usage of this word by the Patrists has been illustrated in the second chapter. It is used a few times in the Septuagint, and, as the Septuagint was in the hands of the Greek-speaking Jews, and is frequently quoted in the New Testament, the usage of the word in that Version calls for attention.

The Greek words bapto and baptizo in the Septuagint have the same general characteristics as in the classics, while baptizo has its special secondary meaning, purification. The differences and resemblances of these words are the same as in classic usage. Bapto has its primary and some of its secondary significations, but in both its primary and in its secondary meanings it is clearly distinguished from baptizo. From the failure to observe this distinction, it has often been treated as if it were employed to denote the rite of baptism. But it is never thus used in the Septuagint or in the New Testament. It is never used as a synonym of baptizo, nor is it ever applied to the ordinance of baptism. It occurs in the following passages: Ex. xii. 22; Lev. iv. 6, 17, ix. 9, xi. 32, xiv. 6, 16, 51; Num. xix. 18; Deut. xxxiii. 24; Josh. iii. 15; Ruth ii. 14; 1 Sam. xiv. 27; 2 Kings viii. 15; Job ix. 31; Ps. lxviii. 23; Ezek. xxiii. 15; Dan. iv. 33, v. 21; also, New Testament, Luke xvi. 24; John xiii. 26; Rev. xix. 13.

In its primary meaning it expresses a specific and definite act, *to dip.* "The priest shall dip his finger in the blood, and sprinkle" (Lev. iv. 6).

"A clean person shall take hyssop, and dip it in the water, and sprinkle" (Num. xix. 18).

It is also used in a secondary sense, as it is in the classics, to express condition. In Ezek. xxiii. 15 it signifies "dyed attire," or, as Prof. Stuart translates it, "colored turbans" (p. 307). This is the same as its classic signification, *to dye.*

Dan. iv. 33, v. 21: "His body was *wet* with the dew of heaven"; or, as Stuart translates it, *moistened*—a meaning which it has in the classics. Dr. Carson (p. 35) contends for the literal meaning. Prof. Stuart translates it "smear or moisten" in Ex. xii. 22 and Lev. iv. 17, xiv. 16, where the Seventy, by using the Greek preposition ἀπό with the genitive case, evidently "meant to give another shade of meaning to the expression" from what they would have done if they had translated by the preposition εἰς—*into*—with the accusative case, as in Lev. iv. 6, ix. 9, xi. 32, xiv. 6, and other places.

As the word bapto in its primary signification is the Greek word employed in actual usage, both in the classics and in the Scriptures, to express the act denoted by *dip;* and as this Greek word is

Baptisms in the Septuagint. 107

never applied to the ordinance of baptism; and as the two Greek words bapto and baptizo are never interchanged with each other; and as there is no need of two words to express exactly the same thing, it is wholly without reason, as well as devoid of examples of usage, to make baptizo have the same identical signification with bapto. The distinction which Greek usage makes between these two words in their respective significations should be kept clear.

SIRACH XXXIV. 30.

Baptizo is not often found in the Septuagint; but its use in Sirach xxxiv. 30 is of eminent value, as it relates, not to a single occurrence, but to *a national custom of daily occurrence* during the whole fifteen hundred years of the life of the Jewish people. By the Law of Moses any person contracted ceremonial defilement by touching a dead body, and he received ceremonial purification by having the water of separation sprinkled upon him on the third day and on the seventh day. This purification Sirach calls a baptism, and millions of these baptisms were performed as generation after generation died and passed away.

The translation of this important passage by

Dr. Dale has already been given. Prof. Stuart gives it the same meaning. He translates the word "*cleansed*": "He who is CLEANSED from a dead [body] and toucheth it again, what does he profit by his washing?" ("Bib. Rep.," Vol. III. p. 308).

As this important passage has given rise to much discussion in respect to some related words, and as these related words have a varied bearing on the subject, I will give a list of them. The Greek word *loutron*, at the close of the quotation, comes from the Greek word *louo*, which the Seventy often use to translate the Hebrew word *rahats*. These words do not denote a specific act, as *to dip*, but they express the generic idea *to wash, to bathe, to cleanse*. The use of the word "wash" and "bathe" in the English Version also requires attention.

1. The Hebrew word *rahats* occurs in the following places: Gen. xviii. 4, xix. 2, xxiv. 32, xliii. 24, 31; Ex. ii. 5, xxix. 4, 17, xxx. 18, 19, 20, 21, xl. 12, 30, 31, 32; Lev. i. 9, viii. 6, xiv. 8, 9, xv. 5, 6, 7, 8, 10, 11, 13, 16, 18, 21, 22, 27, xvi. 4, 24, 26, 28, xvii. 15, 16, xxii. 6; Num. xix. 7, 8, 19; Deut. xxi. 6, xxiii. 11; Judges xix. 21; Ruth iii. 3; 1 Sam. xxv. 41; 2 Sam. xi. 2, 8, xii. 20; 1 Kings xxii. 38; 2 Kings v. 10, 12, 13; 2 Chron. iv. 6 *bis*;

Ps. xxvi. 6, lviii. 10, lxxiii. 13; Prov. xxx. 12; Cant. v. 3, 12; Isa. i. 16, iv. 4; Ezek. xvi. 4, 9 = 65.

This Hebrew word is translated by three Greek words in the Septuagint—*louo*, *nipto*, and *pluno*. These Greek words are also used occasionally to translate other Hebrew words.

2. The Greek word *louo* occurs in the Septuagint in the following places: Ex. ii. 5, xxix. 4, xl. 12; Lev. viii. 6, xiv. 8, 9, xv. 5, 6, 7, 8, 10, 11, 13, 16, 18, 21, 22, 27, xvi. 4, 24, 26, 28, xvii. 15, 16, xxii. 6; Num. xix. 7, 8, 19; Deut. xxiii. 11; Ruth iii. 3; 2 Sam. xi. 2, xii. 20; 1 Kings xxii. 38; 2 Kings v. 10, 12, 13; Ps. vi. 6; Isa. i. 16 = 38.

3. The Greek word *nipto* is used in Gen. xviii. 4, xix. 2, xxiv. 32, xliii. 24, 31; Ex. xxx. 18, 19, 20, 21; Lev. xv. 11, 12; Deut. xxi. 6; Judges xix. 21; 1 Sam. xxv. 41; 2 Sam. xi. 8; 2 Chron. iv. 6; Ps. xxvi. 6, lviii. 10, lxxiii. 13 = 19.

4. The Greek word *pluno* is used in Ex. xxix. 17; Lev. i. 9, xiv. 8, 9, xv. 5, 6, 7, 8, 10, 11, 13, 17, 22, 27; Num. xix. 7, 8, 10, 19, 21; 2 Chron. iv. 6; Isa. iv. 4 = 21.

In the English Version the Hebrew word is sometimes translated *wash* and sometimes *bathe*.

5. It is translated *wash* in Gen. xviii. 4, xix. 2, xxiv. 32, xliii. 24, 31; Ex. ii. 5, xxix. 4, 17, xxx. 18, 19, 20, 21, xl. 12, 30, 31, 32; Lev. i. 9, viii. 6,

xiv. 8, 9, xv. 16, xvi. 4, 24, xxii. 6; Deut. xxi. 6 xxiii. 11; Judges xix. 21; Ruth iii. 3; 1 Sam. xxv. 41; 2 Sam. xi. 2, 8, xii. 20; 1 Kings xxii. 38; 2 Kings v. 10, 12, 13; 2 Chron. iv. 6 *bis;* Ps. xxvi. 6, lviii. 10, lxxiii. 13; Prov. xxx. 12; Cant. v. 3, 12; Isa. i. 16, iv. 4; Ezek. xvi. 4, 9 = 48.

6. It is translated bathe in Lev. xv. 5, 6, 7, 8, 10, 11, 13, 18, 21, 22, 27, xvi. 26, 28, xvii. 15, 16; Num. xix. 7, 8, 19 = 18.

The Hebrew word is translated *wash* nearly three times as often as it is translated *bathe.* "Why our translators have rendered the word *wash* in one case, and *bathe* in another," says Stuart, "it is difficult to see." He adds: "Neither *washing* nor *bathing* appears to be the same as *plunging* or *immersing*" (p. 340). The word is applied to washing the face, the hands, the feet, and sometimes the whole body. It does not express modal action. Nothing depends on the manner of using the water. It does not express a specific act, to dip, but the general idea of washing. It is applied to washing the face in Gen. xliii. 31; the hands in Deut. xxi. 6, Ps. xxvi. 6, lxxiii. 13; the feet in Gen. xviii. 4, xix. 2, xxiv. 32, xliii. 24, Judges xix. 21, 1 Sam. xxv. 41; and the hands and feet in Ex. xxx. 19, 20, 21. Prof. Stuart says: "We find no example among all the Levitical washings or ablutions where immersion of the person is required" (p. 341). Dr. Dale says: "There is no evidence of Jewish ritual purification through all the period of the Law—fifteen hundred years—by dipping the entire person in water" ("Jud. Bap.," p. 366).

THE BAPTISM OF JUDITH.

Judith xii. 7: "And baptized herself in the camp at the fountain of water."

This patriotic lady, the heroine of the story, noted for her beauty, her piety, and her courage, had undertaken the deliverance of her native city, Bethulia, in the north of Palestine, from the siege of the Assyrian army. Making due preparation, she went, accompanied by her maid, to the camp of the enemy. She obtained an introduction to Holofernes, the Assyrian general, and, to cover her design, offered to give him such information that he could easily capture the city. She scrupulously declined to eat at his table, and partook only of her own provisions. She also obtained permission to go out at night into the valley for prayer. As a preparation for prayer, she purified herself by the use of spring-water. This purification was her baptism. The passage is thus translated by Prof. Stuart: "*She went out by night into the valley of Bethulia, and* WASHED HERSELF *in the camp at the fountain of water*" (p. 308). This gives the true meaning. But Dr. Carson translates, "*She dipped herself*" (p. 77). Dr. Conant translates it "immersed herself," and he says: "There was evidently no lack of water for the immersion of the body after the Jewish manner— namely, by walking into the water to the proper depth, and then sinking down till the whole body was immersed" (p. 85).

The signification which these writers claim has not a single circumstance in its favor in the narrative, and it is excluded by the very language of the narrator, and by all the circumstances under which the baptism took place.

1. No act is expressed in the narrative, but the condition of purification is expressed. "She came in clean" (v. 9). As proof has been given from usage, clear, direct, decisive, and abundant, that the word was in current use to denote purification, it will naturally have its usual signification here.

2. The idea of immersion is *excluded* by the very language of the narrator. She baptized herself *in the camp* AT *the fountain*. She did not baptize herself *in* the fountain, but *at* the fountain.

The same identical expression in the Greek is used in chap. vii. 3: "The army camped in the valley near Bethulia, *by* the fountain." In both places the narrator employs the same Greek expression, ἐπὶ τῆς πηγῆς—*at the fountain*. As the army, 170,000 footmen and 12,000 horsemen, did not camp *in* the fountain, but *at* or *by* the fountain, so this Jewish lady did not baptize herself in the fountain, but, as the narrator says, *at* the fountain.

3. As the writer does not say that Judith dipped herself in the spring, but baptized herself in the camp *at* the spring, so the presence of the soldiers *in the camp by the spring* precludes the idea of "the immersion of the body" of this Jewish lady in the fountain. We are informed that Holofernes, a short time previous, "came to the fountains . . . and took them, and *set garrisons of men of war over them*" (vii. 7). With great appropriateness, as well as force, does Prof. Stuart say: "Into the fountain in the midst of the camp it is not probable that she plunged" (p. 308). Dr. Fairbairn says: "Immersion is excluded by the publicity of the scene, as well as by the relation indicated to the fountain" (p. 298).

4. The water of the fountain was used for the purpose of drinking (vii. 13, 20, 21, 22). This in-

creases the *incredibility* of the idea that the fountain would also be used for "the immersion of the body.' The two ideas are incompatible by their very repulsiveness.

5. The water of the fountain was *pure* water, and this gave it the quality requisite for ceremonial purification. Dr. Conant says: "She went to the spring, because she had there the means of immersing herself. Any other use of water for purification could have been made in the tent."

The reply to this is twofold: *First*, if immersion were the object, she could have had enough for that purpose in the tent. *Second*, it was *pure spring*-water that she needed. The quality of the spring-water was the reason why she went to the spring. If she would not even eat the provisions of the Gentiles, neither could the water furnished in Gentile vessels by unclean hands answer the purpose of ceremonial purification. It was a requirement of the Jewish Law that the water for ritual purification should be "living water" (Lev. xiv. 50, 52; Num. xix. 17). Josephus employs the same word *spring* or *fountain* to denote the water required for a ceremonial purification. There is a cleansing quality in pure water by which it has a power to baptize ceremonially or symbolically in whatever way applied.

6. There was a general custom in Oriental countries to wash the hands before prayer, which by Clement is called a baptism. Clement calls the hand-washing of Telemachus a baptism, referring to Homer's statement that "Telemachus, having washed his hands of the hoary sea, prayed to Minerva."

Hesiod admonishes "never with unwashed hands" to worship "Zeus or the other immortals." He also forbids to pass "a stream on foot before washing the hands in it, with prayer" (Smith, "Dic. Christ. Ant.," Vol. I. p. 758).

Ovid teaches "the washing of hands, and the sprinkling of the head with water, before prayer" ("Jud. Bap.," p. 374).

Aristeas says: "It is customary for all the Jews to wash their hands with sea-water when they would pray to God" (p. 374).

Philo says: "It is the custom of nearly all others to sprinkle themselves with pure water, many with that of the sea, some with that of rivers, and some with that which, in vessels, they have drawn up from wells" (p. 374).

Chrysostom says: "It is the custom for fountains to be placed in the courts of houses of prayer, that they who are going to pray to God may first wash their hands, and so lift them up in prayer" ("Dic. Christ. Ant.," I. p. 759).

There is no "Jewish custom of walking into the water to the proper depth, and then sinking down till the whole body is immersed"; but the custom of washing the hands before prayer was an Oriental custom of wide and general prevalence, of which more examples are given in Smith's "Dictionary of Christian Antiquities."

ISA. XXI. 4:
"Iniquity baptizes me."

This is an example of the secondary use of the word, expressing a specific condition, corresponding to the nature of the baptizing power. The specific influence of wine drunk is to *intoxicate*. The specific influence of an opiate drug is to *stupefy*. The specific influence of pure water is to *purify*. The specific influence of iniquity over a person waked up to a consciousness of guilt is to *terrify*. The Hebrew word which the Septuagint translates "*baptize*" means *to affright*. The English Version of the Hebrew is, "Fearfulness affrights me." This condition of terror the Septuagint expresses by the word *baptize*: "Iniquity baptizes me"—*i.e.*, brings me into a condition of terror. We cannot translate the word by a verb of modal action. We cannot say, "Iniquity pours me" (Williams), or "Iniquity dips me," as the theory of Dr. Carson requires. He himself is here obliged to abandon his modal word and say: "His sin . . . *sunk* him in misery," and "would sink him eternally, . . . if not delivered by that which is represented in the baptism of Christians" (p. 86). Even so. The word baptizo does not itself withdraw that which it places under the power of the baptizing element. The condition of baptism has no self-termination. It may continue "eternally." The word does not mean dip—putting an object into a fluid or any element for a moment, and then taking it out; it leaves its object under the power of the element, where it would remain without limit of duration, unless some other influence should take it out of that condition.

In this instance the prophet is describing the scene at the feast of Belshazzar in Babylon, at the time of the capture of the city by Cyrus. As the king gazed upon the handwriting on the wall and read his doom, a consciousness of his guilt sent terror to his heart. "*Iniquity baptizes me,*" "brings me into *a complete condition of terror.*" The passage is easy of explanation on Dale's theory, that baptizo expresses *condition*, the nature of the condition being determined by the nature of the baptizing power.

2 KINGS V. 14:
"Then went he down, and baptized himself seven times in Jordan."

The Hebrew word in this passage is *tabal*, whose primary and most frequent meaning is *to dip*, and so the English Version translates the word. But the Septuagint employs the word *baptizo*, and the question is whether they used the word in this place to denote the definite act *to dip*, or in the secondary signification *to purify*. There are reasons for believing that they used it in the secondary meaning.

1. In all other places where the Hebrew word *tabal* is used in its primary signification, *to dip*, the Seventy use the Greek word *bapto*. They employ bapto to translate tabal in Ex. xii. 22; Lev. iv. 6, 17, ix. 9, xiv. 6, 16, 51; Num. xix. 18; Deut. xxxiii. 24; Josh. iii. 15; Ruth ii. 14; 1 Sam. xiv. 27; 2 Kings viii. 15; Job ix. 31—fourteen times. Bapto, then, is their uniform word elsewhere to express the primary signification of the Hebrew word. The use of a different word in this place indicates a difference in their understanding of the idea to be conveyed. They must have had some reason for choosing this word rather than the other. They rejected the word bapto, *to dip*, and selected baptizo; and for the rejection of the

Baptisms in the Septuagint. 119

usual word and the selection of a different word they must have had a reason in the view they took of the different significations of the two words.

2. This is confirmed by the fact that in other passages they recognized a secondary meaning to the Hebrew word *tabal*, and selected a Greek word that would express the change in the meaning. We have an example of this secondary use of tabal in Gen. xxxvii. 31, where, in the judgment of the Seventy, the Hebrew word tabal has the secondary meaning *to stain*. In that passage they reject the word *bapto* and select the Greek word *moluno, to stain :* "And they took Joseph's coat, and killed a kid of the goats, and stained the coat with the blood."

There are two facts in their translation which show that they did not understand that the coat was "dipped in the blood," as the English Version gives it, but "stained with the blood." *First,* they employ the Greek word *moluno,* whose meaning is *to stain* (Liddell and Scott); *second,* they use the Greek word translated blood in the dative case without the preposition—the *instrumental dative* —to denote the instrument or means by which the coat was stained. In Ezek. xxiii. 15 they use the word *parabapto* in the sense to *dye,* where also the Hebrew word has the same secondary meaning. In 1 Chron. xxvi. 11, the Seventy embody the Hebrew word *tabal* in a proper name. Gesenius translates it, " Whom Jehovah has immersed—*i.e., has purified*" ("Heb. and Eng. Lex.," p. 385). A tendency in the Hebrew word to the meaning *to purify* is thus recognized. The only remaining example is in the passage before us; and the fact that the Seventy employ a change of word elsewhere to express a change from the primary to a secondary meaning confirms the opinion that the reason which induced them here to make a change in the translating word was their understanding of a change in the meaning of the Hebrew word in this place.

3. The prophet Elisha did not employ the word *tabal* in his direction to Naaman (2 Kings v. 10), but the word *rahats*. He did not command him to *dip*, but to *wash*. The Septuagint also translates the command in v. 10 by *louo, to wash*. The same words were used by both Naaman and his servants in v. 12, 13. Dr. Carson at last recognizes the generic meaning of louo: " That the word does not necessarily express mode, I readily admit " (p. 486).

4. It is in proof that the word baptizo means

purify. For all these reasons it may have this meaning here.

In "Theodosia Ernest," American Baptist Publication Society, p. 130, it is said that "tabal is in this Jew Greek uniformly rendered by 'bapto' or 'baptizo,' and these words are never used in any other than their common classical signification."

These statements are both of them erroneous, and indicate the need of more accurate and thorough investigation. *First*, the word *tabal* is translated *moluno* in Gen. xxxvii. 31, with the secondary meaning *to stain*. It is translated *parabapto* in Ezek. xxiii. 15, with the secondary meaning *to dye*. *Second*, the word baptizo is used in the secondary signification *to purify* in unnumbered examples in Hellenistic Greek usage, some of which are cited in the second chapter of this book. The reasons in favor of this secondary meaning in 2 Kings v. 14 are:

1. This is the correct signification of the word in its religious usage, as unnumbered examples demonstrate.

2. This is the meaning of the words employed by the prophet Elisha in his command to Naaman, in Hebrew, Greek, and English, and the same words are repeated by Naaman and by his servant.

3. The Seventy give the Hebrew word *tabal* secondary significations in their translation of it in other places.

4. When the Seventy understand *tabal* to have its primary signification, *to dip*, elsewhere, they uniformly translate it by the Greek word *bapto;* and if they had so understood it here, bapto would have been their word to express it.

5. The selection of *baptizo* in this place *in preference* to bapto shows that they understand *tabal* to have a meaning here which bapto would not express, but which baptizo does express—viz., *purification.*

CHAPTER VI.

SECONDARY MEANING IN THE LEXICONS.

AS the lexicons give the meaning of words, great efforts have been made to make it appear that the lexicons give to the Greek word baptizo only one meaning. The mystification respecting the meaning which the lexicons give to this word is remarkable. A secondary meaning is given in the lexicons; but this, in various ways, is either denied or kept out of view. A brief consideration is, therefore, given to this topic in this chapter.

The secondary meaning of baptizo cannot be precluded by the theory that words have only a single meaning. Some contend with great earnestness for such a theory. The theory does not accord with the reality. Sir William Hamilton says: "Either the words of a language must each denote only a single notion . . . or a plurality of concepts. Of these alternatives, the latter is the one which has been universally preferred; and accordingly all languages by the same word express a multitude of thoughts, more or less differing from each other." President N. Porter, editor of Webster's Dictionary, says: "Without discussing the metaphysical question whether there is or can be more than a single meaning to a word, . . . we accept the commonly-received notion that one word has several senses" ("Bib. Sacra," Vol. XX. p. 119).

Neither can the secondary meaning be precluded by the theory that bapto and baptizo are synonymous in meaning. This theory has been often assumed, but it has never been proved. As an assumption it is very unlikely. If one word has but a short lifetime, another will come in its place; but two words expressing one single idea, existing side by side for several thousand years, are not needed. The best recent lexicographers, whose mature judgment has been formed by the studies of a lifetime, do not favor such a theory. Dr. William Freund, author of the "Latin-German Lexicon," in his very able preface says: "Every word has its own distinct and peculiar meaning. Many words have in their meanings so much resemblance to one another that a superficial examination can hardly distinguish them. It is the duty, therefore, of the internal history of words to hold up the meaning of such words over against one another—to compare and to distinguish them. *This is the synonymous element of lexicography*" (Translation by Pres. T. D. Woolsey, "Bib. Sac.," Vol. II. p. 81). President Porter says: "If no two words have precisely the same meaning—and that they have not is well-nigh demonstrated by the circumstance that two in *fact* exist—then to define one by the other is to confuse rather than to enlighten the mind" (XX. 87). Dr. Dale has thoroughly refuted the opinion that the two words bapto and baptizo are equivalent in meaning.

Neither is the secondary meaning of baptizo precluded by its derivation from bapto. Dr. Dale gives very cogent reasons for deriving it from the secondary meaning of bapto ("Johannic Baptism," p. 64 seq.) Bapto primary denotes a specific act, *to dip;* bapto secondary means *to dye.* This secondary meaning does not express a definite act, but a condition—a condition of color caused by any one of any number of acts that are competent to effect the condition. As the secondary meaning of bapto, so unlike the primary meaning, was determined by examples of usage, so the secondary meaning of baptizo is determined by usage, and *no mere à priori theory* can have any force to nullify the testimony of examples of usage

The testimony of the lexicons to the secondary meaning of baptizo cannot be silenced by merely quoting their testimony to its primary meaning. It is a frequent practice of those who say the word has only one meaning to quote the words that denote the original meaning, and omit those that express the secondary. Dr. Carson is not one of those who take this objectionable course. He wrote a book to prove that the word "has but one signification. . . . *It always signifies to dip; never expressing anything but mode.*" But he says: "I have all the lexicographers and commentators against me in this opinion" (p. 55). Prof. Stuart, also, says that this opinion "in respect to one meaning, and one only," is a position "which every lexicon on earth contradicts, and always must contradict" ("Bib. Rep.," Vol. III. p. 384). Dr. Dale says: "Lexicographers give 'wash' and 'cleanse,' by more than twenty varying or repeated defining terms, as the secondary meaning of this verb" ("Johannic Baptism," p. 62). Dr. Carson, knowing that the lexicons were against him, made his appeal to usage. He says: "It is always lawful to appeal from lexicons to the language itself" (p. 56). This is true, for the meanings of words in the lexicons are obtained from their use in the language; and when for any cause there is a difference of opinion in respect to the meaning given in the lexicons, as in the word baptizo, an appeal to the use of the word in the language to determine its meaning is needful, and, when fairly and fully made, is decisive. How far Dr. Carson succeeded and how far he failed is not here the question. But of the authority of the lexicons he says: "I admit that lexicons are an authority, but they are not *an ultimate authority.* Lexicographers have been guided by their own judgment in examining the various passages in which a word occurs; and it is still competent for every man to have recourse to the same sources. *The meaning of a word must ultimately be determined by an actual inspection of the passages in which it occurs, as often as any one chooses to dispute the judgment of the lexicographers*" (p. 56).

Lexicography is still imperfect. Great improvements have been made in recent years, but the ideal of a perfect lexicon has not yet been reached in any language. The most intelligent and appreciative admirers of the best and latest lexicons of the Greek, Latin, and English languages do not claim perfection for any one of them, but acknowledge existing defects, and point them out with a view to improvements yet to be made. The most important element in a lexicon is the definition. In this element has been one of the deficiencies of the past, and in it is one of the great improvements which the makers of dictionaries are exerting their best efforts to attain. The very ideal of a good definition is one of the ripe results of a recent period. In treating of this subject President Porter says: "It is the duty of the definer, first, to be well assured that he has collected all the senses of his words; then that he has expressed them in well-thought and adequate phrases; and then that he has arranged them in the order of their development and historic growth." He insists that a definition "in ordinary cases cannot be given by a single word," but must be given "in well-chosen language, by a compact and clearly-uttered proposition" ("Bib. Sac.," Vol. XX. pp. 92, 119). The defects in the lexical definitions of the Greek word baptizo have been often felt, but the attempts to remedy them have not been very successful. Dr. Carson selected the single word "dip" to express the meaning, but was often obliged to abandon it for words that differ essentially in signification, as "sink" and the equivocal word "immerse." Dr. Conant, in his definition, employs seven different words which are far from being exact equivalents. Dr. Dale has discussed the subject with great ability, and has done what has never before been done for a revision of the definition. He has fully explored the original sources, and gathered all the passages, not only in classic but in Judaic and Patristic Greek, in which the word occurs, and with philosophic insight has discerned and developed the several meanings of the word, the primary and the secondary, in the natural order of their growth. (See "Johan. Bap.," pp. 59-68; "Jud. Bap.," p. 57; "C. B.," p. 354).

President Porter says: "The definitions should be illustrated by quotations. . . . Words are made for sentences; they have their life and meaning from their connection; and it is only as seen in living and connected discourse that their import or use can be fully understood. By all means, then, let us have illustrative quotations, given freely and variously" ("Bib. Sac.," XX. 121). In the second chapter of this book nearly a hundred quotations are given from the works of Dale, in which the word baptizo occurs more than a hundred times in the secondary meaning—purification—besides other quotations in other chapters, and the number could easily be doubled. Most of these quotations are so clear and decisive that they must carry conviction to every mind that gives them fair consideration. They put it in the power of each one to form an independent judgment of his own. The quotations are the primary source of knowledge on which the lexicons are founded. But the lexicons, though secondary in authority, possess a value which will justify a few citations from such as are held in high estimation. It is said that sixty lexicons were quoted in a recent debate on baptism. Whether more enlightenment or more bewilderment ensued does not appear. A selection of original quotations from the works of Dale, with the testimony of a few of the best lexicons fairly considered and duly weighed, would be sufficient to determine and settle the secondary meaning. The testimony of a few of the numerous lexicons which give this meaning is here presented.

1. Robinson, in his "Greek and English Lexicon of the New Testament," the standard lexicon in use in this country and in other parts of Christendom, after referring to its classic use, gives as its meaning in the New Testament *to wash, to lave, to cleanse by washing, to administer the rite of baptism;* and he gives four reasons to show that "in Hellenistic usage, and especially in reference to the rite of baptism, it would seem to have expressed not always simply *immersion*, but the more general idea of *ablution* or *affusion.*"

2. Scapula, in his "Greek and Latin Lexicon," having given the primary meaning *mergo*, etc., also gives the secondary meaning, *abluo, lavo.* What does *abluo* mean? We turn to the "Latin-English Lexicon" of F. P. Leverett, "compiled from the lexicons of Facciolati and Forcellini, Scheller, Luenemann, and Freund," and observe that it gives as the definition of *abluo, to wash, to wash off, to make clean, to purify.* The definitions given of *lavo* are *to wash, to bathe, to besprinkle, to bedew.*

3. Wahl gives as its second meaning νίπτω, *lavo.* What does νίπτω mean? Liddell and Scott define it *to wash, to purge, to cleanse, to purify.*

4. Bretschneider, who draws his illustrations more from Hellenistic Greek than some lexicographers, who draw more from classic Greek, gives as its first meaning *lavo, abluo,* to *purify*.

5. Schleusner gives as its second meaning *abluo, lavo, aqua purgo.* We will turn this time to the "Latin-English Lexicon" of E. A. Andrews, founded on the "Larger Latin-German Lexicon of Dr. William Freund." This lexicon defines *abluo, to remove filth by washing, to wash away, to cleanse or purify.* It defines *lavo, to wash, bathe, lave; to wet, moisten, bedew; to wash away.* And it defines *purgo, to make clean or pure, to clean, cleanse, purify.*

6. Suidas gives . . . *lavo, abluo, purgo, mundo.* Andrews defines *mundo, to make clean, to clean, to cleanse.*

7. Parkhurst gives as one of its secondary meanings, *to baptize, to wash in or with water in token of purification from sin.*

8. Hermann Cremer, professor in the University of Greifswalde, in his "Biblico-Theological Lexicon," the latest which has appeared in Germany, translated in Edinburgh, and introduced into this country (bearing date 1872), p. 418, says that "βαπτίζειν was used for the New Testament washing in order to purification," and that "λούειν serves in some passages to give prominence to the full import of βαπτίζειν, which had become a technical term, or (as in Rev. i. 5) to denote purification generally."

9. Other lexicons give the definition *abluo, to purify,* among which are the eminent names of Schrevelius, Hedericus, Stockius, Schoetgen, Suicer, and others.

CHAPTER VII.

BIBLICAL SCHOLARS.

THE opinions of eminent Biblical scholars are entitled to respectful and thoughtful consideration. Sometimes, however, an undue reliance is placed upon the authority of great names. When good and learned men differ in opinion, we must exercise the primal right and duty of every man to consider the reasons of a just opinion, if we would arrive at the essential truth.

Immersionists have often put forth the claim that they have all the learning and scholarship that is worthy of respect in favor of the opinion that the Greek word baptizo has only one meaning, *to immerse*. This claim has no foundation, and has no weight with those who are well informed, and who look beyond mere opinions to the evidence. Nor would it here be noticed were it not for the misrepresentation which is often made of the views of eminent scholars who do not believe in the theory of "one meaning, and one only," to this word. The use which is made of the name of Prof. Stuart is especially surprising.

Moses Stuart has been called "the father of sacred literature in this country." As the leader in that revival of Biblical study whose influence is now felt in every land, he will be held in immortal honor. As he made the Word of God the supreme authority for his own religious belief, so he sought to arouse the minds of his pupils to the earnest and independent study of the inspired volume, in the free exercise of their powers, accountable only to its Author. His chief excellence as an instructor consisted in awakening an enthusiasm in the interpretation of the Scriptures by the best methods and for the highest and most sacred purposes. He did not teach his pupils to rely merely on his opinions, but to test all opinions by the Word of God, making use of all the helps which can aid in the understanding of its meaning. He expected there would be progress and improvement in the knowledge of Biblical subjects after his time. Yet his name adds weight to the views which he published to the world. This has been a temptation, which some immersionists have not been able to resist, to claim him on their side of the baptismal question. In his treatise on the "Mode of Baptism"

Biblical Scholars. 135

he went to the bottom of the subject, and gave first the original signification of the word, and then gave the secondary meanings. But in numerous instances they have quoted what he says on the original meaning of the word, and have suppressed what he says of the other meanings, representing him as teaching that the word has only one meaning.

Prof. Stuart's article on the "Mode of Baptism" was published in the third volume of the *Biblical Repository* in 1833, and republished the same year in a pamphlet. In giving some of his testimony to the secondary meaning of baptizo, references will be made to the pages of both. In each reference the first number will refer to the page in the *Repository*, the second to the page in the pamphlet.

1. Prof. Stuart teaches that baptizo has *more* than *one* meaning.

Under "Classical Usage" he discusses the meanings of both words, bapto and baptizo, and, having given their first meanings, *dip, plunge, immerge, sink,* he says: "But there are variations from this usual and prevailing signification"; and, after giving illustrations, he says: "In all the derived or *secondary* meanings of *both* bapto and baptizo . . . the Greek writers made a diverse and distinct use of the words, never confounding them" (p. 306; p. 22).

Under "Septuagint Usage" he says: "Some of the classical meanings of these words are not to be found in the books aforesaid; while *other meanings*—viz., *to wash, to bedew or moisten*—are more clearly and fully exhibited" (p. 308; p. 24).

As he says of the first meaning: "All lexicographers and critics of any note are agreed in this," so of the theory that the word has "one meaning, and one only," he says it is a position "which every lexicon on earth contradicts, and always must contradict" (p. 384; p. 100).

2. Prof. Stuart teaches that the meaning of baptizo in its religious usage is *purification*.

Among the several meanings in the Septuagint he gives: "5. *To wash, cleanse by water*, where baptizo is used" (p. 308; p. 24).

He gives the same meaning in his translations:

Judith xii. 7: "*She went out by night, into the valley of Bethulia, and* WASHED *herself in the camp at the fountain of water.*"

Sirach xxxiv. 30: "*He who is* CLEANSED *from a dead* [*body*], *and toucheth it again, what does he profit by his washing?*"

In Judith he translates baptizo *washed*, in Sirach *cleansed*.

Tit. iii. 5: "*He saved us by the* WASHING [loutron] *of regeneration—i.e.*, by that purification which regeneration confers" (p. 337; p. 53).

The word *loutron*, which Stuart translates *washing* in Sirach and Titus, and explains in Titus as signifying *purification*, is the word which Sirach employs to denote the meaning of his expression, "He who is baptized from a dead body."

Eph. v. 26: "*Having cleansed it by the* WASHING [loutron] *of water by the word.*"

Acts x. 47: "Can any man forbid water, that these should not be baptized?" This Stuart explains: "Can any one forbid that *water should be brought in?* . . . They were to be baptized on the spot, and water was to be brought in for this purpose" (p. 334; p. 50).

In summing up the result of an extended discussion he says: "Let us return to the rite of baptism. What is it that it signifies? *Purification* is the answer; and this is the only Scriptural and consistent answer that we can give" (p. 367; p. 83).

3. Prof. Stuart does not believe that baptism consists in the *mode*.

"The mere *mode* cannot possibly make any difference in the case" (p. 388; p. 104).

"*No injunction is anywhere given in the New Tes-*

tament respecting the manner in which this rite should be performed. If there be such a passage, let it be produced. This cannot be done" (p. 365; p. 81).

The opinion that "the manner of the rite is involved in the word itself" Prof. Stuart rejects, and shows that the mode is not involved in the meaning of the word. He devotes twenty pages to the argument in proof that the mode of baptism is not essential.

4. Prof. Stuart believes that baptism with water is a *symbol* of the purification of the soul by the Spirit of God.

He says there is a "twofold division of the external ritual under the ancient dispensation and under the Christian one—viz., into *rites emblematic of purity, and rites emblematic of atonement for sin*" (p. 370; p. 86). On p. 369, p. 85, he says: "Under the ancient dispensation, the rites were divided into two great classes—viz., *those significant of purity or purification, and those significant of atonement for sin.* . . . Are not the significant symbols, then, under the new dispensation, a summary of those which existed under the old? The belief of this spontaneously forces itself upon my mind. The work of the Spirit is still symbolized under the Gospel; and a Saviour's blood is still represented. The one *baptism* signifies; the other is as plainly indicated by the Lord's Supper."

5. Prof. Stuart rejects the error "that baptism is a symbol of the death and burial of Christ."

It represents the purification of the soul by the Spirit of God. "It is a dying to sin and being raised to a new spiritual life. . . . Why should baptism be made symbolical of the *death* of Christ? All Jewish analogy is against it. What were all the ablutions and sprinklings of the ritual law designed to prefigure and to signify? Most obviously we must answer, *purification*. . . . Water, as exhibited in washing, sprinkling, etc., is never an emblem of death and the grave" (p. 368; p. 84).

Of Rom. vi. 4, 5 and Col. ii. 12 he says: "It is only *moral* or *spiritual* baptism into the death of Christ of which the apostle speaks in these two passages" (p. 370; p. 86).

"It is perfectly clear that baptism is considered as the symbol of purification. . . . It is significant of that sanctifying influence of the Spirit of God which a Saviour's death has procured" p. 368; p. 84).

6. Prof. Stuart maintains that immersion is not essential as a mode of baptism, but that sprinkling

is a valid and the most significant and appropriate mode.

"Is it essential, in order that baptism should symbolize *purification or purity*, that it should be performed by immersion? Plainly not; for in ancient times it was the water which was *sprinkled* upon the offending Jew that was the grand emblem of purification" (p. 370; p. 86).

"It is, then, a perfectly clear case that the *sprinkling* of water or of blood was altogether the most significant mode of purification under the ancient dispensation. And so the prophet Ezekiel speaks of water to be *sprinkled*, under the new dispensation—Ezek. xxxvi. 25, 26" (p. 371; p. 87).

"After the examples which have been adduced of the *significancy of sprinkling*, both from the Old Testament and the New, . . . I consider this significancy as a point made out" (p. 372; p. 88).

Of certain passages in the New Testament which he discusses he says: "I cannot read these examples without the distinct conviction that *immersion* was not practised on these occasions, but *washing* or *affusion*" (p. 362; p. 78).

He concedes the "probability" that the rite was sometimes performed by immersion, but the main drift of his argument is in favor of sprinkling, of the validity of which he has no doubt, and the greater appropriateness and significancy of which he conclusively evinces. Near the conclusion he says: "My belief is that we *do obey* the command to baptize when we do it by affusion or sprinkling" (p. 388; p. 104).

7. In treating of the mode of baptism in the early ages of Christianity *after* the times of the apostles, Prof. Stuart says that immersion was the general practice, but that sprinkling was also considered valid. He quotes a long passage from Cyprian, and says: "Here, then, *sprinkling*, so early as the former half of the third century, is pronounced to be legitimate and valid by one of the noblest men among all the Christian fathers.... This noble and liberal decision of Cyprian was confirmed and proclaimed by several ecclesiastical councils not long afterwards" (p. 379; p. 95).

Prof. Stuart thinks undue stress is laid by immersionists on the practice of the early churches. "If this be authoritative, then why not be consistent and carry it through?" (p. 382; p. 98). "It is notorious, and admits of no contradiction, that baptism in those days of immersion was administered to men, women, and children, *in puris naturalibus*, naked as Adam and Eve before their fall" (p. 381 : p. 97). Numerous other superstitious observances, he also shows, would be obligatory on that view.

There is much false reasoning about the testimony of church history on the subject of baptism. R. Robinson's "History of the Baptists" is still quoted by a certain grade of writers. Of this book Prof. Stuart says: "I have examined it on various topics, and confess myself to be greatly disappointed and not a little disgusted. There is everywhere in it an air of almost *profane levity*, which at times breaks forth into the most gross and *palpable indecency*. . . . There is such a gross and palpable unfairness in Robinson's examination of the testimony of the Christian fathers, and such a shallow criticism both on them and on the New Testament, that one may well wonder that this book should meet with encouragement among men of sobriety and good sense. There is, indeed, an appearance of a kind of learning in the author; but it is merely that of a literary *gourmand*, who has read everything curious and entertaining, and but very little that is solid, *and has reasoned and reflected still less on what he has read*" (quoted in "Woods on Infant Baptism," 2d ed., p. 140). Some recent critics would become wiser if, instead of depending on such discredited authorities as R. Robinson, they would resort to genuine and trustworthy sources of information on this subject.

Alexander Carson, the ablest defender of the theory of "one meaning, and one only," to the Greek word baptizo, was a contemporary of Moses Stuart, but inferior to him in some of the essential qualities of a successful interpreter. His definition of baptizo is a lucid statement of the meaning given to it by the theory: "*It always signifies dip*, never expressing anything but mode." This definition expresses exactly the meaning of bapto primary, but it does not express the meaning of baptizo. The first fallacy in Dr. Carson's reasoning consists in transferring to the word baptizo, without evidence, the primary meaning of bapto, *to dip*, assuming that they are equivalent in signification. Underlying this assumption, and connected with it, is the further assumption that baptizo must express some definite act, *to sprinkle*, *to pour*, or *to dip;* and therefore, like bapto, it must mean *dip*. This is the original fallacy which warps and vitiates all the subsequent reasoning in favor of the theory. The first two examples which Dr. Carson gives furnish illustration of this fundamental error in his conception of the meaning of the word. Of the quotation from Polybius, "They marched through with difficulty, the infantry being baptized up to the breasts," he says, p. 57: "Here surely the word cannot mean *pouring or sprinkling.*" Therefore he infers that as the word must denote *some* definite act, and as the act is not that of pouring or sprinkling, it must be the act of *dipping*. But there is no action expressed by the word baptizo in this quotation. The action, and the *only* action, which Polybius expresses, is the act of *marching*, and this action is expressed by another and a different word. *Wading through a river* is quite a different thing from the act of dipping an object in the river. The word baptizo does not express the action, but it expresses the *condition* of the soldiers *in the water* while marching through the river. The word dip expresses an entirely different idea. In the next example, where Strabo says: "The army marched through the entire day, baptized up to the waist," Dr. Carson says: "Surely this baptism was immersion." Here comes another fallacy. Why does he shift the word, and substitute "immersion" for "dipping"? The word dip denotes a definite act, "to put for a moment in any liquid." But a whole day is too long for the momentary act, *to dip*. Besides, the only act of which Strabo speaks is the act of marching, and this is expressed by a different word. There is no action in the word baptizo in either of these examples. The baptism was an immersion, but the immersion was not an act, but the *condition* of the *soldiers in the water*. Dr. Carson had not considered the difference in the meaning of the two words. When he comes to the baptism of ships, he substitutes the word "sink" for "dip." The ships have been in a condition of baptism for more than a thousand years, but that is too long a period for the duration of the act which is expressed by the word dip, which Dr. Carson has put into his definition, and he employs another word of different meaning.

The baptism in Isa. xxi. 4, "Iniquity baptizes me," he also expresses by the word "sink," and says it might continue "eternally" (p. 86). The word "immerse" in English, like the corresponding word in Latin, sometimes denotes an act, but, apart from the baptismal question, it more frequently expresses *condition* without limit of time. The following examples will illustrate this:

"After *sixty years*' immersion, the gold looks as fresh as if taken out of the bank."

"The lamp extinguished, he was immersed in total darkness."

"*Immersed* deep in the flood, he found the death he had deserved."

To substitute the word "immerse" for the word "dip," as if they were equivalent in signification, serves only to mislead. The word "dip" expresses a momentary act—"entrance into a fluid, with immediate return." The word "immerse" expresses condition which continues for a long period of time.

Dr. Carson conducts his argument on the principle that no second meaning of the word shall be admitted until some example is adduced in which the first meaning is *impossible*. He often encounters passages which tax his critical powers to the utmost to find some possible way of explaining them in accordance with his theory. He expends a vast amount of ingenuity to reduce intractable passages to "one meaning, and one only." Of one notable example he says: " I have found that *baptizo* in other instances signifies to *immerse*, and there is a certainty that it has this meaning here, except it is proved that it has another signification somewhere else. If another signification is found, I will not insist that immersion *must of course* be the signification here " (p. 452). But he never allows that " it has another signification somewhere else"; therefore in no case is the secondary meaning to be admitted. For he adds: "*Now, there is not in all Greek literature a single instance ever alleged in which this word* MUST *have a secondary meaning.*" This is Dr. Carson's potent weapon of defence when he meets with passages which give him special difficulty in their conflict with his theory. It often leads him into as great extravagance of interpretation as that which he himself exposed when he rejected the notion, which had been maintained during many generations, that the Homeric lake was literally dipped in the blood of a mouse. Since Dr. Carson's day a great number of passages have been adduced by Dr. Dale which to Dr. Carson were wholly unknown. Some of these are given in the second chapter of this book. It is wholly unnecessary here to repeat the argument there given from examples of usage. They fully meet the demand of Dr. Carson's principle. In the greater part of these examples *it is impossible* to give the word its primary meaning, but from the *very nature of the case the word* MUST *have the secondary meaning—purification.* The lexicographers are right. They have substantiated this secondary meaning, and no attempt to suppress or deny or reverse their judgment can succeed. The appeal which Dr. Carson made from the lexicons to the usage of the word has failed to disprove the secondary meaning, while subsequent and more complete investigation has established that meaning on a stronger and broader foundation.

Dr. Carson, like most immersionists, failed to distinguish between the classical and the Hellenistic significations of the word. In its secular use in the classics, while it has both primary and secondary meanings, the secondary meaning, purification, is rare. But in its religious usage, as appropriated by the Greek-speaking Jews to denote ceremonial purification, and also the spiritual purification of the soul by the Spirit of God, and the symbol baptism with water by which the spiritual is ritually represented, this is the prevailing signification in Judaic, Johannic, Christic, and Patristic baptisms.

Dr. T. J. Conant, BAPTIZEIN, ed. 1868, has published for the American Bible Union the result of his investigation of this word. He employs seven words to express its meaning: *to immerse, immerge, submerge, to dip, to plunge, to imbathe, to whelm* (p. 87). These words differ much from each other in meaning, yet they unite in the common idea "that the object was wholly covered by the enclosing element" (p. 159). He selects the word *immerse* for use in his Revision of the translation of the New Testament. On p. 101 he says: "The Greek word BAPTIZEIN expresses nothing more than the act of *immersion*"; and on p. 88 he says: "The word *immerse* . . . expresses the full import of the Greek word BAPTIZEIN. The idea of *emersion* is not included in the meaning of the Greek word. It means simply to put into or under water (or other substance), without determining whether the object immersed sinks to the bottom, or floats in the liquid, or is immediately taken out." So far as the simple meaning of the Greek word extends, it leaves its object in the enclosing element, and does not of itself determine that it shall be "taken out." The idea of "taking out" of the water the object which is "put into or under water," by the Greek word baptizo, is an idea which is not contained in the meaning of this word, and is not expressed by it. If there be not some other cause to withdraw the object from the watery element, how is it ever to be "taken out"? What shall determine the taking of the object out of the water in any case? "This is determined not by the word itself." But if "the word itself" does not determine the withdrawal of its object; if in its own intrinsic meaning, and by its own proper agency, it does not withdraw its object from the water; if this word does not itself, in its actual, current Greek usage, express the *taking out* as well as *the putting in;* if we must resort to motives and reasons *extrinsic* to "the word itself," then "the act" on which Dr. Conant insists as essential to Christian baptism is not denoted by this Greek word. The word itself does not determine whether the object which is "put into or under water" is to be "taken out." He says: "This is determined, not by the word itself, but by the nature of the case, and by the design of the act in each particular case. A living being, put under water without intending to drown him, is of course to be immediately withdrawn from it." The potent motive involved in the natural desire to avoid drowning, to which the phrase "of course" adroitly points, will doubtless incite to take a living being out of the water, if he has been "put under the water." But the Greek word baptizo, *in its classic usage*, does not take out of the water what it puts in. "The idea of emersion is not included in the meaning of the Greek word." In the New Testament the Greek word baptizo never puts a living being under the water.

Dr. Conant is a distinguished scholar, and holds an honorable position as the leading translator of the Baptist Revision of the English Version of the New Testament. He has collected a goodly number of quotations from Greek writers in BAPTIZEIN, and says that these "exhaust the use of this word in Greek literature" (p. vi.) In this he was greatly mistaken, as hundreds of new examples in the works of Dr. Dale attest. The Greek text of Dr. Conant is carefully and accurately edited, but his translations and explanations are often unsatisfactory. His punctuation of the Greek text in his example 221 differs from that of the best authorities, like the Abbé Migne of Paris, and is evidently erroneous, and his translation still more so.

Dr. James W. Dale, of Media, Pennsylvania, in his "Inquiry," has given the Greek word baptizo a more complete and scientific investigation, with a result more luminous and satisfactory, than any other scholar. When Prof. Stuart wrote his treatise in 1833, the amount of material accessible to scholars in this country was very limited. A half-century of discussion, of research, of intense mental activity, has given a vantage-ground to those who have the enterprise to seize the opportunity. The incessant and fruitless debate of the baptismal question has revealed its weak point. Dr. Dale has had the sagacity to discover that weak point, and, grasping the great principle that "Use is of supreme authority and the rule in the language," he has explored the whole realm of Greek literature, and has found "the key which opens every passage" and discloses its meaning. He has collected, classified, and expounded all the examples in which the word occurs in classic Greek, all known examples in Judaic Greek, and a multitude in Patristic Greek, hundreds of which were never seen by Dr. Carson or by Dr. Conant. He has had the enterprise to procure from Europe the original works in the best and most approved editions, and has made his quotations with a fairness and an accuracy which have commanded the commendation of the intelligent among those who differ most widely from him in opinion. His four splendid volumes, Classic, Judaic, Johannic, Christic and Patristic Baptism, have received the encomiums of the most eminent Greek scholars in the United States, and awakened respectful attention from the most intelligent advocates of immersion. His views have received endorsement from forty universities, colleges, and theological seminaries, through more than sixty of their professors and presidents, and his works are hailed by Christian scholars as a full, thorough, complete, and satis-

Biblical Scholars.

factory treatment of the Greek word baptizo. His works are a thesaurus of information on the subject, and his discussion of it cannot fail to exert a potent influence for the elimination of error and the establishment of the truth.

CHAPTER VIII.

JEWISH BAPTISMS IN THE NEW TESTAMENT.

I COR. X. 2: "BAPTIZED INTO MOSES."

WHEN the Israelites stood trembling with the Red Sea before them, the impassable mountains on either side, and the hostile army of Pharaoh fiercely menacing them behind, in their terror and unbelief they poured their reproaches upon Moses for leading them out of Egypt, as they said, "to die in the wilderness"; and they declared that they would rather "serve the Egyptians" than go on thus to inevitable destruction. But when, the next morning, they stood safe on the other shore, and beheld the destruction of the Egyptians and the great deliverance which God had given to them by the hand of Moses, their state of mind was entirely changed. Now "the people feared the Lord, and believed the Lord and his servant Moses." There was in them a thorough change. They were *baptized into Moses*. The day before, appalled by the terrors that encompassed them, they were almost in a state of rebellion. But now there was a complete change. The whole nation had been baptized into Moses—changed from a state of unbelief into a state of confidence in Moses and devotion to him as their leader. This baptism had been accomplished by the divine interposition through the instrumentality of the cloud and the sea. "The pillar of the cloud went from before their face, and stood behind them: and it came between the camp of the Egyptians and the camp of Israel; and it was a cloud and darkness to them, but it gave light by night to these: so that the one came not near the other all the night" (Ex. xiv. 19, 20). Thus the pillar of the cloud was a terror to the Egyptians and an illumination and protection to the Israelites, so that they passed over between the divided waters of the sea to the opposite shore on dry ground. The effect of this great deliverance upon their minds, bringing them into subjection to the leadership of Moses, was what the apostle calls their baptism: "They were all baptized into Moses by the cloud and by the sea."

The efforts to explain this passage on the theory that the word denotes some specific modal act—to dip, to sprinkle, or to pour—have not been successful. They do not conform to the historical facts that pertain to this baptism. The theory that the word denotes a thorough change of condition is the one which explains the facts, and is sustained by them. The modal theory does not conform to the historical facts.

The advocates of each of the three forms of the modal theory seem to think that the word must mean either one or another of these acts, *to dip*, or *to sprinkle*, or *to pour;* and, on this theory, the enquiry is, In which of these three acts does the baptism consist? Is it dipping, or pouring, or sprinkling? R. S. Poole, in his article on the passage of the Red Sea, in Smith's " Dictionary of the Bible," edited by H. B. Hackett, Vol. III. p. 2692, says: " At the time of the passage of the sea there was a storm of rain with thunder and lightning (Ps. lxxvii. 15-20). To this St. Paul may allude (1 Cor. x. 2); for the idea of baptism seems to involve either immersion or sprinkling, and the latter could have here occurred; the reference is evidently to the pillar of the cloud." Others also, as Fairchild (p. 27), Peters (p. 63), Beckwith (p. 16), give the same view: " Water was sprinkled upon them from the cloud. It passed over them, and, in passing, rained upon them, and thus baptized them." Dr. Gill, who held that the word means *to dip*, says that the cloud, as it passed from the front to the rear of the camp, "let down a plentiful rain upon them, whereby they were in such a condition as if they had been all over dipped in water" (Barnes in loco, p. 196). Hall (p. 73) says: "If there is any *mode* of baptism here, it is a *sprinkling*, or such a *pouring out* of water as falls in drops. A baptism there was; an immersion there was not."

There are two decisive objections to the theory that water was poured or sprinkled upon the Israelites from the cloudy pillar. *First*, the pillar was not a rain-cloud. It was the Shekinah, the pillar of cloud by day and of fire by night, which sometimes stood above them, sometimes went before them, sometimes behind them, for their guidance and protection. *Secondly*, the pillar had *already* passed over them and taken its position *behind* them before they entered the Red Sea, and it remained behind them and between them and the Egyptians during the whole night. An appeal is made to Ps. lxxvii. 17: "The clouds poured out water." But here it was the *clouds*, not the pillar of the cloud; and the tempest was sent, not upon the Israelites, but upon the Egyptians, against whom the "arrows"—*i.e.*, the lightnings—were shot from the thunder-cloud. The Israelites were under divine protection. "Thou leadest thy people like a flock by the hand of Moses and Aaron" (v. 20). The expression in Judges v. 4, "The clouds also dropped water," to which Dr. Peters refers, relates to the region of Seir and Edom, a different locality. The "plentiful rain," Ps. lxviii. 9, to which he also appeals, was at Sinai.

Beckwith, Peters, and Fairchild also say that the baptism "in the sea" was by sprinkling. The "strong east wind" blew the spray from the waters foaming around them, and dashed it upon them. But the record says nothing of this, and the wind was blowing the waters away from them. Dr. Carson says: "It was a real immersion. The sea stood on each side of them, and the cloud covered them" (p. 119). When reminded that the Israelites went through on dry ground he replies: "They got a dry dip" (p. 413). But the Israelites were *not covered* by the cloud when they passed through the sea. It had gone behind them before they commenced their march, and remained behind them all the night. There was nothing above them but the open sky. This fact, that before they started on their nightly march, and during the whole night, the pillar of the cloud was behind them, and not over them, is fatal to the modal theory in every form. It unroofs Dr. Carson's nicely-constructed baptistery, which at best was but a tunnel open at both ends, and leaves nothing but the march of the people in open space over dry ground. The only "action" was the tramp, tramp, tramp of the moving hosts. The idea of immersion, and of sprinkling by the dashing of the spray, is each a mere fancy. There were two millions of men, women, and children, with all their flocks, and herds, and tents, and household goods. Even in the compact form of Robinson ("Biblical Researches," Vol. I. p. 84), in columns of a thousand persons abreast and two thousand in depth, the body must have been half a mile in breadth and not less than two miles in extent, occupying at least four hours in the passage. The larger estimate is more probable, that they spread out a mile in width and five miles in depth. Any estimate is fatal to the dipping theory, and to the theory that the spray of the sea was sprinkled over all that vast host of people. The "dry dip" of Dr. Carson is the culmination of the fancies of the modal theory.

Dr. Carson further says that the baptism "resembled the baptism of believers," and "served a like purpose as attesting their faith in Moses as a temporal saviour." But this statement is in direct opposition to the historical fact as related by Moses. The passing through the sea was not appointed for the purpose of *attesting* their faith in Moses, but for the very opposite purpose of *inducing* faith in Moses. Before the passage, they were sadly lacking in faith and were almost in despair. Their safe passage, secured by such remarkable instrumentalities as the pillar of the cloud and the divided waters of the sea, was the cause by which their unbelief was removed and their faith in Moses established.

One thing by which Dr. Carson and others have been misled is the failure to consider the chronological order of the events. Paul enumerates five of the events in the order of their occurrence. *First*, "All our fathers were under the cloud." This was *before* they entered the Red Sea (Ex. xiv. 19, 20). *After that*, Moses stretched out his hand over the sea and the waters were divided, and then, in the words of Paul, they "all passed through the sea." But *before* they started the cloud *had passed to their rear*, and remained there to protect them from the Egyptians while on the passage. As the *result* of their passage through the sea, they "were all baptized into Moses by the cloud and by the sea." The effect of their safe passage was to produce confidence in Moses, and devotion to him as their leader. The next event in order which Paul enumerates is the gift of the manna for food in the wilderness: "And did all eat of the same spiritual meat." The event next mentioned was still later in the order of time: "And did all drink of that same spiritual drink: for they drank of that spiritual Rock that followed them: and that Rock was Christ." These events are narrated in the order of time. If the theorists had noticed the chronological order of the events, they would not have placed the cloudy pillar *over* the people as a covering while on the passage through the sea, when it was *behind* them to protect them from the Egyptians.

There was no immersion of the Israelites. The Egyptians were immersed, and, if their immersion be called a baptism, it was a destructive baptism. By the cloud they were baptized into terror, and by the sea they were baptized into destruction. But the Israelites were baptized into Moses by the safe passage of the sea, as they "went over dry shod." Thus "they were all baptized into Moses by the cloud and by the sea."

The English Version translates "in the cloud and in the sea." But the translation "by the cloud and by the sea," as Dale renders it, is the true one. It is supported, *first*, by the fact that the cloud and sea were instrumental agencies in securing the safe passage of the Israelites; *secondly*, by the fact that the cloud and the sea were not the elements into which they were baptized, but they were baptized into Moses; *thirdly*, the translation "in the cloud" does not convey the meaning of the apostle; he does not mean to locate them in the cloud; they were not enveloped in the cloud; the cloud never did envelop the people, but it always either stood above them or went before them or behind them; they were not immersed in the cloud, nor were they immersed in the sea, but the cloud and sea were the instrumentalities by which their safety was secured; *fourthly*, the Greek preposition is frequently used in the New Testament to denote instrumentality, and is often translated by words that signify instrumentality; *fifthly*, the preposition is translated "by" in passages that refer directly to the pillar of the cloud, as in Nehemiah ix. 12: "Thou leddest them in the day *by* a cloudy pillar, and in the night *by* a pillar of fire"; Ps. lxxviii. 14: "In the daytime, also, he led them *with* a cloud, and all the night *with* a light of fire"; also in Ps. lxxvii. 20: "Thou leddest thy people like a flock *by* the hand of Moses and Aaron."

In the same way the Patrists understand and represent this baptism ("Jud. Bap.," pp. 292, 304).

Hilary says: " Per mare et per nubem purificati "—They were purified (baptized) *by* the cloud and *by* the sea.

John of Damascus calls it, " That baptism which is *by* (διά) the cloud and the sea."

Basil, in direct terms, says: " But the sea and the cloud, at that time, *induced faith* through amazement; but, as a type, it signified, for the future, the grace that should be after."

Thus Basil ascribes to the cloud and the sea the instrumental agency of producing faith in the people.

Didymus Alexandrinus: " The waters, securing safety for the people, signify baptism."

It was by the instrumentality of the waters in "securing safety for the people" that they signify baptism.

Didymus also says: " The whole material of their journey from Egypt was a type of the salvation by baptism."

Baptism, as he represents its type, has nothing in it of modal action, but was the permanent condition of the people.

DAILY BAPTISM BEFORE MEALS.

Luke xi. 37, 38: "And as he spake, a certain Pharisee besought him to dine with him: and he went in, and sat down to meat.

"And when the Pharisee saw it, he marvelled that he was not first baptized before dinner."

The word baptized, as here used by Luke, was so well understood by his readers that they needed no explanation of its meaning. It related to a practice of constant, daily occurrence. It was not a mere physical washing, but a customary ritual cleansing which the Jews observed at the time of their daily meals. What this custom was we learn in Mark vii. 3: "The Pharisees, and all the Jews, except they wash their hands oft, eat not"; and in Matt. xv. 2: "Thy disciples . . . wash not their hands when they eat bread." The time in the last two passages was a few months later, but the custom referred to is the same as in Luke—the customary ablution at meals. This baptism before eating was not enjoined in the law of Moses, but in the tradition of the elders; and it was omitted by Jesus on this occasion, and by his disciples on the subsequent occasion. "Why do thy disciples transgress the tradition of the elders? for they wash not their hands when they eat bread."

The ablution was performed by washing the hands. The Pharisee noticed the neglect of this customary baptism on the part of Jesus, and manifested his surprise at the omission. This gave occasion for the reproof which Jesus administered to him for such an observance of a mere external ceremony, and for his neglect of internal purity. "Ye Pharisees make clean the outside, . . . but your inward part is full of . . . wickedness."

Theophylact, in his comment on this passage, says of Jesus: "Deriding their foolish custom— I mean their purifying themselves before eating— he teaches that they ought to purify their souls by good works. For washing the hands purifies the body only, not the soul" ("Johannic Baptism," p. 117).

Robinson, in his "New Testament Lexicon," article "Baptizo," gives four reasons in proof that the word in Hellenistic usage expressed "the more general idea of ablution or affusion." The first of these reasons is drawn from this Jewish baptism thus: "This appears from the following consideration: (*a*) The circumstances narrated in Luke xi. 38, compared with those in Mark vii. 2–4, where *nipto* is employed, implying, according to Oriental custom, a *pouring* of water on the hands."

The word *nipto*, which Mark uses to describe this rite, is also used by Theophylact in his comment on the baptism in Luke xi. 38, and its meaning is, " *to wash*, but only some part of the body, as the face, hands, feet" (Rob. "Lex.")

Alford says: "This use of the word shows that it *did not imply necessarily the immersion of the whole body;* for it was only the hands which the Pharisees washed before meat."

BAPTISM FROM THE MARKET.

Mark vii. 4: "And except they baptize themselves from the market, they eat not."

This is a literal translation by Dr. Dale, who compares it with similar forms of expression in Sirach, Clement, Justin Martyr, and in the New Testament, deducing, by a clear and critical exposition, the meaning, "purify themselves from the market." The ceremonial defilement which the Jews contracted in the market they removed before eating by the customary ablution. The previous verses show that this was done by washing the hands. If we take only the New Testament and its surroundings, the nature of this baptism is sufficiently plain. It was a ceremonial purification by washing the hands.

But Dr. Carson says: "It ought to have been

translated, 'Except they dip themselves, they eat not'" ("Baptism," p. 68). His argument is that "the word signifies *to dip*, and only *to dip*" (p. 67), and therefore it "must" have that meaning here. On p. 452 he says: "I have found that baptizo in other instances signifies to *immerse*"; and he argues: "There is a certainty that it has this meaning here, except it is proved that it has another signification somewhere else." But what if it be proved that it has another signification somewhere else? "If another signification is found, I will not insist that immersion *must of course* be the signification here." Now, it *has been proved* from passages without number that the word has another and a very different meaning. It has the secondary meaning *to purify*. This completely reverses the argument as urged by Dr. Carson. As Dale would say: "It is in proof that the word has the secondary signification to cleanse" in religious usage; it therefore has this signification here. Dr. Dale wields this argument in "Johannic Baptism" with convincing force. It is not needful here to amplify this argument.

The general prevalence of the custom of washing the hands for ceremonial purification *confirms* the interpretation of this hand-washing baptism.

I. Ceremonial purification by washing the hands was an Oriental custom from generation to generation. Dr. William Smith, in his "Dictionary of Christian Antiquities," Vol. I., article "HANDS, WASHING OF," gives numerous examples from the Old Testament, from Hesiod and other classic writers, from Tertullian, Chrysostom, Cyril, and other Patristic writers, in illustration of this custom.

II. One of the most frequent methods of this ceremonial purification was by *pouring* water on the hands.

1. Robinson, "N. T. Lex.," p. 481, says: "The usual mode of ablution in the East is by pouring water upon the hands; this is done by a servant."

2. In 2 Kings iii. 11: "Here is Elisha the son of Shaphat, which poured water on the hands of Elijah."

3. When Dr. E. Robinson was in Hebron, Palestine, in May, 1838, in a house where ten persons dined "in the true Oriental style," as he relates in his "Biblical Researches," Vol. II. p. 451, one of the persons "went and washed his hands by having water poured upon them in an adjacent room." Another "did not leave his place to wash, but had the water brought to him where

he sat." In June, when Dr. Robinson and Rev. Eli Smith were at Ramleh, they accepted the proposal of their host "that a servant should wash our feet." The servant "brought water, which she poured upon our feet over a large, shallow basin of tinned copper; kneeling before us, and rubbing our feet with her hands, and wiping them with a napkin" (Vol. III. p. 26).

4. Dr. Thompson, describing an Oriental meal, says: "Their pitcher and ewer are always brought, and the servant, with a napkin over his shoulder, pours water on your hands."

5. Hilary, A.D. 354, intimates of one place where they did not "pour water on the priest's hands, as we see in all the churches" ("Dic. Christ. Ant.," Vol. I. p. 759).

6. Rabbi Akiba, when the water which the jailer brought to him in prison was not enough to drink, said: "Pour the water on my hands; it is better to die with thirst than transgress the tradition of the elders" (Poole's "Synopsis," Fairchild, p. 20; Dale, p. 104).

III. The ceremonial purification of the person by washing the hands is called baptism by the Patrists.

Ambrose, in his comment on the passage in Mark vii. 2-4, says: "The Jews, in following the tradition of men, neglect that of God; the disciples, in giving precedence to that of God, neglected that of men, so that they would not wash their hands when they ate bread—since ' he who is completely washed has no need that he should wash his hands' (John xiii. 10). Jesus had washed them: they sought no other baptism; for Christ by one baptism resolves all baptisms" ("Johannic Baptism," p. 102).

They did not need that other baptism by washing the hands, for the one perfect baptism which they had received from Christ was sufficient.

Clement of Alexandria, quoting the hand-washing of Telemachus as a baptism, says: "This [hand-washing baptism] was a custom of the Jews, so as even to be baptized frequently upon the couch" (p. 103).

The couch upon which Clement says the Jews were frequently baptized according to custom, was the couch on which they reclined at meals.

Theophylact also calls the washing of the hands a baptism (p. 117).

IV. The Jews had in their houses the means of ceremonial purification. "And there were set there six *water-pots* of stone, *after the manner of the purifying of the Jews*, containing two or three firkins apiece" (John ii. 6). A log containing less than one gallon was a sufficient quantity, according to the Jewish estimate, for the legal purification of a single person. Even a quarter of a log was sufficient to wash the hands of one or two persons (Smith's " Dic. of the Bible," Vol. IV. p. 3507; Lightfoot, in Dale, p. 104).

BAPTISM OF COUCHES.

Mark vii. 4: "And there are many other things which they have received to hold—the baptizings of cups, and pots, and brazen vessels, and couches."

The couches which the Jews baptized were the table couches, on which they reclined at meals. The great size of these dining couches, on a single one of which several persons could recline, puts the dipping theory of Dr. Carson to a severe strain. Yet he says: " Though it were proved that the couches COULD NOT BE IMMERSED, I would not yield an inch of the ground I have occupied" (Carson on "Baptism," p. 76). Among the suggestions he makes to escape the difficulty, he thinks it possible that the beds which the Pharisees baptized were " the beds on which they slept." But the baptism of the couches is mentioned in connection with their meals, and the word has its usual signification of a dinner couch.

But the doctor says: "Whatever might have been their size, they might easily be immersed in a pond. . . . I have contrived to take them to pieces" (p. 400). So we might take a house to pieces, and dip it, piece by piece. But such airy fancies are not worth the chase. The fact that the word "has been proved" to have a secondary meaning takes it wholly out of the region of fanciful possibilities, and places it on historic ground. The only method of purifying household goods spoken of in the Old Testament is by sprinkling—Num. xix. 18: "A clean person shall take hyssop, and dip it in the water, and sprinkle it upon the tent, and upon all the vessels"; and although the dinner couch is not specified, and therefore cannot be proved to be included among the vessels, yet it is one of the articles of domestic furniture, and belongs to a class that were purified by sprinkling. We are sometimes referred to Num. xxxi. 23. But this relates to an ordinance of war concerning articles obtained from foreign sources, which, from their pre-eminent uncleanness, required an unusual purification. This is the only instance in the Bible where even material objects were required to be purified by immersion. This was never the ordinary mode of purification. " Sprinkling," says Prof.

Stuart, "was used most frequently of all by way of purification" ("Bib. Rep.," Vol. III. p. 339). Alford says: "These baptisms as applied to κλίνων [meaning probably here couches (trichnia) used *at meals*] were certainly *not immersions*, but sprinklings, or affusions of water."

HEB. IX. 10: "DIVERSE BAPTISMS."

The word "washings," by which the Greek word *baptisms* is translated in the English Version, expresses the true meaning; for these baptisms were *cleansings, washings, purifications*. But this version does not apprise the English reader that those washings are baptisms. If the word had been translated *baptisms*, it would have directed the attention of the reader of the English Version to the baptisms of the Old Testament.

The apostle teaches that there is a diversity of these baptisms. He also speaks of baptisms in the plural in Heb. vi. 1 : " The doctrine of baptisms"; but he does not there refer to Judaic baptisms, as he does in Heb. ix. 10. These baptisms are diverse in their nature; in the agencies by which they are effected, and in the mode of accomplishment. There were various baptismal agencies, such as sacrificial blood, heifer-ashes, and water, and these diverse agencies had a di verse power, and, in their operation, induced diverse conditions—*i.e.*, diverse baptisms.

The Patrists often speak of a diversity of baptisms. Hilary says: "Baptismata sunt diversa," under which heading he speaks of the baptism of John, the second baptism of Christ, the baptism of the Spirit, the baptism of fire, of judgment, and the baptism of martyrdom. Thus diverse, both in their agencies and modes of operation, are the baptisms of which he makes enumeration. Ambrose describes six kinds of baptisms. He says: "Multa sunt genera baptismatum"—*There are many kinds of baptisms;* "Plurima baptismatum genera"—*Very many kinds of baptisms.* The theory that there is only one baptism—viz., a specific act, *to dip*—is an invention of later times.

Basil says: "We should learn, in brief, the diversity between the baptism of Moses and that of John."

Chrysostom says: "John exhorted the Jews not to cherish hopes of salvation through diverse baptisms and purifications of waters."

Justin Martyr says: "The law released from blame, daily, transgressors by certain sprinklings . . . and diverse kinds of baptisms, but grace grants only one baptism."

Gregory Nazianzen: "Come, let us enquire

something concerning the difference of baptisms, that we may go hence purified." He enumerates and describes six different baptisms ("Jud. Bap.," p. 380).

The baptisms of the Old Testament of which Paul speaks included the purifications by sprinkling the blood of bulls and goats and the ashes of a heifer. He specifies these on account of their emblematic nature. He is making a comparison between the Mosaic and the Christian dispensations, and especially between the purifications of the Jewish ritual and the great purification which Jesus Christ made for men by his death on the cross, of which those Jewish baptisms were a type.

The "diverse baptisms" include the purifications by sprinkling the sacrificial blood and heifer-ashes mentioned in v. 13. The "carnal ordinances" in v. 10 consist of the "meats and drinks and diverse baptisms"; and as those purifications are not found in the "meats and drinks," they must be included in the "baptisms."

1. The word "and" before "carnal ordinances" in the English Version is not in the original. It is not in the Greek text of Robinson's edition of the New Testament by Augustus Hahn, 1842, nor in that of Tischendorf, 1873.

Both editions note it as a variation, but reject it from the genuine text. It is not even recognized by Stuart, Winer, and other scholars.

2. Consequently, the word "ordinances" is in apposition with "meats and drinks and diverse baptisms," explanatory of them, and therefore includes them. Stuart shows this in his translation: "*Meats and drinks and diverse washings—ordinances pertaining to the flesh*" ("Commentary," p. 431). Winer also, in his "New Testament Grammar," p. 635, says that the word "ordinances is in apposition to meats and drinks and diverse baptisms." In another remark he calls it "that appositive word." Prof. Stuart says: "Meats and drinks and diverse baptisms I understand as a clause qualifying ordinances—*i.e.*, these words stand in the place of an adjective designating wherein the ordinances consisted." Prof. Wilson says: "The term 'carnal ordinances' does not express something additional to the *meats* and *drinks* and *baptizings*, but is another name for the same ritual observances" ("C. and P. B.," p. 332). Dr. Dale says: "That 'the diverse baptizings' are included in the 'carnal ordinances' (ordinances of the flesh) is a matter of universal acknowledgment" ("Jud. Bap.," p. 385).

3. The description which Paul gives of the

ritual efficacy of "the blood of bulls and of goats, and the ashes of a heifer"—an efficacy which merely consists in "purifying the flesh"—places them among the ordinances of the flesh; and as they do not belong to the "meats and drinks," they must be found in the "diverse baptisms." They are called "ordinances of the flesh" because they only sanctify "to the purifying of the flesh," as the Patrists say, "having power, for the time, for the purification of the body." They are external, ceremonial ordinances, ritual purifications, typical of the greater purification by the sprinkling of the blood of Christ. "For if the blood of bulls and of goats, and the ashes of an heifer, sprinkling the unclean, sanctifieth to the purifying of the flesh, how much more shall the blood of Christ, who through the Eternal Spirit offered himself without spot to God, purge your conscience from dead works to serve the living God?"

In full harmony with this doctrine of the apostle is the testimony of the Patrists.

Ambrose says: "He who wished to be cleansed by typical baptism was sprinkled with the blood of the lamb by a bunch of hyssop" ("C. and P. B.," p. 534).

Hilary: "But sprinkling according to the

Law is the cleansing from sin through faith purifying the people by the sprinkling of blood (Ps. l. 9)—a sacrament of the future sprinkling of the blood of the Lord" (" The Cup and the Cross," p. 34).

Ambrose: "For he who is baptized, whether according to the Law or according to the Gospel, is cleansed : according to the Law, because Moses sprinkled the blood of the lamb with a bunch of hyssop; according to the Gospel, because the garments of Christ were white as snow " (p. 34). The ashes of a blood-red heifer Paul also represents as typical of the blood of Christ. In this view the testimony of Moses, Josephus, Philo, Cyril, and Gregory Nazianzen, to the ceremonial purification of the unclean by sprinkling the ashes of a heifer, has great value. Gregory Nazianzen says : " Therefore let us be baptized, that we may overcome; let us partake of the purifying waters . . . more sanctifying than the ashes of a heifer sprinkling the unclean, and having, for the time, power for the purification of the body, but not for the complete removal of sin " (p. 34). The complete removal of sin is effected only by the blood of Christ. " The type-baptism of Judaism," says Dale, "contemplates the purification of the body from ceremonial defilement. This purification of the body, as a ceremonial effect, was perfect. It was, therefore, well adapted to be a type of the purification of the soul by the blood of Christ. The blood of bulls and goats, and the blood-red heifer-ashes, are universally regarded as types of the blood of Christ. . . . We have the clear and unanimous interpretation of these early writers for the identification of Jewish and Christian baptisms, as type and antitype baptism, as well as the unerring authority of inspiration, through Paul, for conjoining the diverse baptizings of the Old Testament (especially its sprinklings) with that one wondrous and central baptism of the new dispensation—THE BAPTISM OF CALVARY." (p. 32).

CHAPTER IX.

BAPTISM WITH WATER.

John i. 26: "I baptize with water."

FOUR centuries had passed since the latest of the Hebrew prophets had foretold the coming of Elias. When the people heard the voice crying in the wilderness, they knew that he had come. The whole Jewish nation was moved by his ministry. This distinguished preacher received a commission from heaven to announce the Messiah and prepare the people to receive him. To give a fitting reception to the coming One, a great change was requisite in the character of the people. To promote this preparation was the mission of John the Baptist. A thorough reformation was needful, and this was set forth by preaching the baptism of repentance into the remission of sins. This repentance-baptism was symbolized by an external rite—the baptism with water.

Pure water is the natural symbol of moral purification. In all nations and in all ages it is the prime agent for cleansing, and the first and main symbol of purity. The purifying quality of water makes it a fit emblem of the purification of the soul by the Spirit of God. Baptism is twofold, spiritual and ritual; the one real in the soul, the other an emblem, a shadow of the real. The baptism of John partook of this twofold nature. The baptism which he preached was the baptism of repentance into the forgiveness of sins, a spiritual change in the condition of the soul; the baptism which he administered was a baptism with water, emblematical of the baptism of repentance. The baptism of repentance was a change in the character and spiritual condition of the people, and this inward change was symbolized by an external rite administered to those who had become subjects of the spiritual change.

This twofold baptism of John in its purifying nature was understood and described by Josephus: "For Herod slew him [John the Baptist], a good man, exhorting the Jews to cultivate virtue, and observing uprightness toward one another and piety toward God, to come for baptizing [purification]; for thus the baptizing would appear acceptable to him, not using it for the remission of sins, but for purity of the body, provided that the soul has been previously purged by righteousness" ("Johannic Baptism," p. 125).

In this description of John's baptism Josephus gives his knowledge of its nature and design, and also "the current popular understanding" respecting it. The soul must first be purified by righteousness, and this condition of the soul is fitly represented by the baptism of the body; and both the one and the other Josephus describes as a purification.

The secondary meaning of the Greek word baptizo, denoting a condition of purification, was in daily, current use in the time of John the Baptist. The proof of this has already been given, and need not be here repeated. The result of an exhaustive investigation of the various baptisms of Judaism is thus given in the conclusion of Dale's "Judaic Baptism," p. 400:

"JUDAIC BAPTISM *is a condition of* CEREMONIAL PURIFICATION *effected by the* WASHING *of the hands or feet, by the* SPRINKLING *of sacrificial blood or heifer-ashes, by the* POURING *upon of water, by the* TOUCH *of a coal of fire, by the* WAVING *of a flaming sword, and by divers other modes and agencies, dependent in no wise on any form of act or on the covering of the object.*"

During the whole period of the Hebrew commonwealth, for fifteen hundred years from Moses to John, those ritual purifications which the Greek-speaking Jews called baptisms were in daily, constant practice. The principal baptismal agencies were sacrificial blood, heifer-ashes, and pure water; and these baptismal agencies were usually applied by sprinkling or by pouring water on the hands. With the nature of these various Jewish baptisms John the Baptist was well acquainted. The secondary meaning of baptizo, expressive of purification, was its common, daily signification in the popular language of the Jews, and had been for several generations. . From the time that Jewish Greek became their vernacular tongue this word had been applied to denote these Hebrew purifications, just as other Greek words had been appropriated to express their Hebrew ideas. All the surroundings of the son of Zacharias from his childhood had been pervaded by the atmosphere of this religious usage. The word was prepared for his use by its whole religious history. The only modification of its meaning which was needed was to turn it from its ceremonial and typical application so as to adapt it to its spiritual and symbolic use in his preaching as the forerunner of Christ. This modification was both needful and natural under the moulding influence of the new order of things.

As the baptisms of Judaism were diverse, so the baptism of John had its own distinctive nature, in which it differed from Judaic baptism. Judaic baptism purified the body ceremonially; John's baptism was a superior baptism. It was the baptism of repentance into the remission of sins, symbolized by a ritual baptism with pure water. The ritual baptism of John was a symbol of the baptism of the soul by repentance. The generic idea common to Judaic and Johannic baptisms was *a condition of purification resulting from some baptizing power capable of producing such a condition.* The character of the baptism in either case was determined by the characteristic of the baptizing agency. It was the characteristic of sacrificial blood and heifer-ashes to produce ceremonial purification. It was the characteristic of pure water, in its ritual use by John, to produce symbol purity, emblematical of the spiritual purity of the soul resulting from the baptism of repentance. But the essential idea common to all these baptisms—purification—received a more elevated and spiritual significance, and a new and fresh life, in the baptism of John.

As the baptism of John was, in its specialty,

different from Judaic baptism, he employed a new word to express it. The word βάπτισμα, the Greek noun which is used to express the baptism of John, appears for the first time in connection with his ministry. It does not occur in any previous writing. It is worthy of special notice, because it belongs to a class of Greek words which do not express *act*, but *effect, a condition* resulting from the action of the verb. This principle is well understood by Greek scholars, but its importance and value in relation to the true meaning of baptism will justify the citation of some proof.

Dr. Dale, "Johannic Baptism," p. 141, says: "Substantives derived from verbs ending in *ma* are used to express the *effect, result, product, state* induced by the verb. In this view all grammarians concur."

Crosby, "Greek Grammar," sec. 364, says: "Nouns formed by adding *ma* to the stem of the verb denote the EFFECT or OBJECT of the action."

Hadley, "Greek Grammar," sec. 461, D, *a*, says: "The RESULT of an action is expressed by the suffix *ma*."

Kühner says: "Substantives with the ending *ma* denote the *effect or result* of the transitive action of the verb."

Winer says: "The most numerous formations are those in *ma*, ... mostly in the sense of *product or state*"; and he gives this very word βάπτισμα as the first example ("N. T. Gr.," Thayer's edition, p. 93).

Sophocles, Jelf, and Philip Buttmann lay down the same principle. Dr. Dale has the most solid reasons for saying: " Baptism (βάπτισμα) denotes *a result, an effect, a condition* from the act of the verb. . . . The use of this word originates in the Scriptures. It is there used to express exclusively a *spiritual* result, effect, or condition. It never has water as its complement" ("The Cup and the Cross," p. 5).

Baptism with water is a symbol of the baptism of repentance. It would be an error to interpret the expression, "I baptize with water into repentance" (Matt. iii. 11), as teaching that baptism with water is "the instrumental cause" of repentance; for water has no power to cause repentance. This interpretation is refuted by the continued impenitence of numbers after receiving ritual baptism. The ritual baptism is but a symbol, an expressive symbol, and useful as such, but without power to produce the change of spiritual condition which it symbolizes. This is seen in the contrast which John presents in this and parallel passages between baptism with water and the baptism of the Holy Ghost. John regarded the Pharisees and Sadducees as unfit candidates for his baptism in their impenitent condition. Others, "confessing their sins," he baptized. As they had experienced the reality, it was fit that they should receive the symbol. But the external rite would be vacated of its meaning and become an empty form to those who did not repent. He therefore said to them: "I indeed baptize you with water into repentance"—simple water, a mere symbol, having no efficacy in itself, but expressive of the repentance which is required—"but He that cometh after me is mightier than I. . . . He shall baptize you with the Holy Ghost and with fire." They must become subjects of the baptism of repentance which John preached, and "bring forth fruit meet for repentance," or baptism with water would be of no avail.

The emblematical character of John's baptism appears in the answer which he gave to a question respecting the nature of his baptism. The enquiry was not, as in the English Version, "Why baptizest thou?" but, as it was understood by the Patrists and by recent scholars, "What [baptism] dost thou baptize?" (Dale, p. 145). John replies:

"I baptize with water," a symbol baptism. There is One coming who "shall baptize you with the Holy Ghost." The baptism of the Mightier One is the real baptism, of which mine is only an emblem. Ambrose, quoting John's language, "I baptize with water," says: "For the body is purified by water; the sins of the soul are cleansed by the Holy Ghost" (Dale, p. 148).

The design of John's baptism involves its emblematic character. Pointing to "the Lamb of God that taketh away the sin of the world," he says: "But that he should be made manifest to Israel, therefore am I come baptizing with water." John's baptism, both the spiritual and the ritual, had its signification in its relation to Him of whom John was the forerunner. "The object of the rite was to direct the attention of the people not only by words, but by the additional help of a visible symbol, to the Lamb of God as in himself most pure, as vindicating the divine purity by his work, and as demanding and securing purification in all who should share in· the fruits of that work. The rite was designed by the use of symbol water to set forth PURIFICATION FROM SIN as the great and vital thought connected with and effected by the coming LAMB OF GOD" (p. 229).

There is a theory very different from this—a theory which denies that the word denotes purification, and declares that it signifies a dipping into water, and that this act of dipping into water is designed to set forth the burial and resurrection of Christ.

But of baptism in any relation to the burial of Christ there is not a syllable in the four Gospels, or in the Acts of the Apostles, or in any writer for more than a quarter of a century after the resurrection of Christ. The first allusion to it is in a metaphorical passage in two of Paul's Epistles, which will be considered in another place.

But it is said the expression in the Greek is ἐν ὕδατι—*in water*—and that this presents the water not as "the means by which," but as "the element in which," the baptism takes place. In "Theodosia Ernest," American Baptist Publication Society, p. 88, we are told: "So you will find it in every place"; and on p. 96 we are told that this is "the true rendering" in Acts i. 5. But the Greek preposition does not occur in Acts i. 5, and where it does occur it is used in the instrumental sense, "with water," as it is correctly translated in the English Version.

1. The Greek word ὕδατι is used in the dative

case *without the preposition* in Acts i. 5, and elsewhere in the New Testament, as the *instrumental means* of baptism. In Acts i. 5, where our Saviour says: " John truly baptized with water "— a passage occupying a position of special prominence in the teaching of Jesus—the simple dative is used without the Greek preposition. It is what the Greek grammarians call *"the instrumental dative."* Prof. Hackett translates it " with water," and in this case even Dr. Conant consents (p. 100). No other translation is consistent with usage. Winer, in his " New Testament Grammar," p. 216, places Acts i. 5, xi. 16, with other passages, under the "dative of the *instrument* (casus instrumentalis)," and translates " with." On p. 412 he translates the expression *"baptize with water."* The word is used in the dative without the preposition to denote the means with which the baptism is performed in Acts i. 5, Acts xi. 16, Luke iii. 16, and, in Tischendorf's New Testament, in Mark i. 8. These examples are sufficient to establish the instrumental signification.

2. The word is sometimes used in the *instrumental* sense *with* the preposition. It is thus used in Matt. iii. 11; John i. 26, 31, 33; and, in Hahn's New Testament, in Mark i. 8.

The use of the preposition in the instrumental sense is very frequent in Hellenistic Greek. Alexander Buttmann, in his "New Testament Grammar," translated by J. H. Thayer, 1873, under "Dative of the Instrument," p. 181, says: "The preposition ἐν is prefixed to this dative with uncommon frequency" in "the language of the New Testament"; and on p. 329 he says: "Ἐν in the Old and New Testaments is very commonly used . . . to designate the *means*." We are told in "Theodosia Ernest" that there are "only about forty places" in the New Testament in which the Greek preposition must be translated "*with* in the sense of the instrument or material with which anything is done" (p. 89). But this, like the statement respecting Acts i. 5, must be numbered among the errors of that theological romance. Even from the Baptist Version of the Bible, which naturally gives only the minimum of examples, Dr. Dale quotes, from the single Gospel of Matthew, thirty-seven passages in which that Version gives it the instrumental sense, "*with*," "*by*," "*through*." He also quotes more than thirty examples from the Book of Revelation in which the Baptist Bible gives it the instrumental sense; and in the whole New Testament, from personal examination, he says the number "must be computed by hundreds" (p. 171). Dr. Dale also gives numerous quotations from Hellenistic Greek writers in the Septuagint and elsewhere of the use of the preposition in the instrumental sense. His statement, like that of Prof. Buttmann, rests upon the solid basis of facts when he says, p. 213: "*It is in proof* that ἐν is used in the classics, and abundantly in the New Testament, in the sense *with, by.*" While, therefore, the Greek preposition in the Septuagint and in the New Testament often means *in*, it also with equal frequency denotes the instrumental means, and is rightly translated "with" in the English Version.

3. A special argument for the instrumental sense is found in the *true reason* for the *variable* use of the two forms of expression in the New Testament. Luke invariably omits the preposition; Matthew and John insert it. Mark omits it, according to the Sinaitic manuscript and Tischendorf's New Testament. Origen quotes both Mark and Luke as omitting it, while he quotes Matthew and John as inserting it (Dale, p. 288). Alford accepts the reading of Tischendorf. Dr. Conant (p. 100) acknowledges "the *instrumental dative*" in Luke iii. 16, Acts i. 5, xi. 16; yet he translates "*in the Holy Spirit,*" in the same passages,

"as the element in which the baptism is performed." The reason which he gives is that "the Holy Spirit could less properly be conceived as the mere instrument of an act." But this reason is not satisfactory. It would require uniformity in the expression relating to water in the Greek in all the passages. It does not account for the *variation* in the different writers. The true reason is given by Prof. Buttmann. Luke wrote more in *the classic style*, which generally employs the simple dative to denote instrumentality. Matthew and John wrote in conformity with *the idiom of the Hebrew*, which very frequently employs the preposition in the instrumental sense. Prof. Buttmann, "New Testament Grammar," p. 329, says: "The Greek preposition ἐν in the Old and New Testaments is very commonly used, *like the preposition beth* in Hebrew, to designate the *means*"; and on p. 181 he says: "This New Testament peculiarity," the uncommon frequency with which the preposition ἐν is prefixed to the instrumental dative, "is manifestly a result of the frequent occurrence of the preposition in the Septuagint, after the example of the Hebrew *beth*, as is apparent from countless examples from the Old Testament and New." The same principle is given by Winer,

"New Testament Grammar," p. 388. In classic Greek instrumental agency is expressed by the dative without the preposition. Of twenty-six such passages in classic Greek in which the word baptizo is used with the simple dative, Dr. Conant translates by the use of the English prepositions "*with*," "*by*" in twenty cases, and might as well have done so in the other six. These passages are quoted by Dale (p. 208). The Greekly style of Luke is the true explanation of his use of the dative of means without the preposition. The Hebraistic style of Matthew and John equally accounts for their use of the preposition in the instrumental sense in conformity with the Hebrew idiom. Dr. Campbell, of Aberdeen, recognizes this Hebraistic use of the preposition, " which, answering to the Hebrew *beth*, may denote *with* as well as *in*" (Dale, p. 158). The variation in the omission or insertion of the preposition before " water " in the Greek, *when truly accounted for*, gives a decisive argument for the instrumental sense. Prof. Buttmann (p. 182) cites Matt. iii. 11 among the examples of " the addition of the preposition ἐν to the instrumental dative," and, in explaining, says " not *in* water." The English Version gives the true meaning by the translation " with " in each class of cases. This interpretation also brings the writers into harmony with each other.

4. The comparison which the Patrists make between baptism with water and baptism with blood gives the instrumental sense: "Thou dost baptize me with water, that I may baptize thee for myself with thy blood" (Jerome). "They were baptized, not with water, but with their own blood" (Bassillius). The Greek preposition is used in the instrumental sense before both water and blood. As one's own blood is not "the element in which," but the agency "by which," his baptism of blood is effected, so water in the corresponding phrase is the agency or "means by which" the baptism is performed.

5. Several other Greek prepositions which denote *means*, as $\delta\iota\acute{a}$, $\dot{\upsilon}\pi\acute{o}$, etc., are used by the Patrists with the Greek words *water*, *blood*, *tears*, *fire*, and other baptismal agencies, as instrumental in producing various baptisms. The use of these prepositions excludes the signification "dipping into." Dale gives the examples (pp. 209, 233, 241, et passim).

PLACES OF BAPTISM.

Matt. iii. 6: "And were baptized of him in Jordan."

Mark i. 5: "Were all baptized of him in the river of Jordan."

The use of baptizo in connection with the place of baptism, especially the river Jordan, is urged as an argument for immersion. But this argument, like the preceding, fails to establish the meaning claimed.

1. The preposition is used to denote simple locality. It signifies "*in* any place, *on, at, by*" (Robinson, "New Testament Lexicon").

2. It is used to denote locality in connection with the word baptizo: "John did baptize in the wilderness" (Mark i. 4). The wilderness was not "the element in which" John baptized the people, but the place where he baptized them. It denotes simple locality. He also baptized in other places—"in Bethabara beyond Jordan" (John i. 28, x. 40), in Ænon (iii. 23), and elsewhere. There were numerous localities where baptism was performed, as Jerusalem, etc. Nothing can be determined respecting the mode of baptism from the local use of the preposition.

3. The river Jordan is a locality, and is spoken of as a locality in connection with baptism: "Then cometh Jesus from Galilee upon [$\dot{\epsilon}\pi i$] the Jordan unto John, to be baptized of him" (Matt. iii. 13). Justin Martyr speaks of Jordan as a locality:

"While John yet dwelt upon [ἐπί] the river Jordan, Christ came." . . . "And Jesus having come upon [ἐπί] the river Jordan, where John baptized" (Dale, p. 376). Dr. Carson, p. 351, says: "When we wish merely to designate the place of baptism, we always use *in*." Prof. Harrison gives this preposition the meaning *at*, *on*, *near*, and illustrates by such examples as Herod., i. 76: "A city *on* [ἐν] the Euxine Sea"; Xen., "Anab.," iv. 8, 22: "A Grecian city *on* [ἐν] the Pontus Euxinus" (Dale, p. 352). Gesenius and Rosenmuller give it the same local signification in connection with rivers and streams. Dr. Dale gives several examples in which it is used to denote locality in rivers and seas, yet not in the water. Dr. Carson, discussing the passage in Homer's "Iliad," xviii. 520, which represents an ambuscade of soldiers as lodging in the river, says: "It was within the banks of the river that the ambuscade lodged" (p. 338). The soldiers had a fine, dry camping-ground in the river between the banks where they could lie in wait. Of Ulysses, who, escaping from shipwreck, lodged all night in the river under shelter of the bank, Dr. Carson also says, p. 339: "He might be *in the* RIVER, *yet not in the* WATER; *all within the banks is the river*." People, then, might be in the river, and be baptized in the river, and not go into the water. There is ample room between the upper bank of the river Jordan and the lower bank, a distance of an eighth of a mile—forty rods—where a multitude of people could stand and be baptized without going into the water. The testimony of travellers makes this plain. Maundrell says: "After having descended the outermost bank, you go *about a furlong* on a level strand before you come to the immediate bank of the river" (Dale, p. 373). Another says: "The Jordan may be said to have two banks, of which the inner marks the ordinary height of the stream, and the outer its elevation during the rainy season" (p. 325).

4. When the word baptizo is used in its *primary classic* signification with the Greek preposition ἐν to denote a baptism, the baptized object REMAINS *in the element*, and is not taken out of it.

Josephus: "And there, according to command, being baptized in a pool by the Galatians, he dies." Whiston translates it "was drowned" ("Wars of the Jews," i. 22, 2).

Polybius: "Baptized and sinking in the pools, . . . many of them perished" ("Classic Baptism," p. 258).

Plotinus: "She dies; . . . and death to her,

while yet baptized in the body, is to sink in matter, and to be filled with it" ("C. B.," p. 264).

The soul remains in the condition of baptism, and is changed to corruption by the influence of the body upon it.

Alexander Aphrodisias: "Baptized in the depth of the body" ("C. B.," p. 264).

This Greek writer thus expresses the death of the perceptive power:

"In this class of baptisms, in every case, without exception, the baptized object is not taken out of the element, but remains within it" ("Johannic Baptism," p. 368). The word, therefore, is not used in the New Testament in its primary signification in connection with the Greek preposition. It is not to its use in the classics that we must look for its meaning, but to its secondary use in the Jewish Greek spoken in Palestine. Dr. Carson and Dr. Campbell lay no stress on the preposition, for they well know that its use affords no evidence of dipping the person into water. Dr. Carson's argument is wholly different. His argument is this: "There can be no adequate cause alleged for going to the river," except for the purpose of immersion (p. 126).

But there is no intimation of this reason, and no fact supporting it, in the narrative. On the other hand, a good reason for baptizing in this locality is found in the fact that "his peculiar character as a witness led him to make the wilderness bordering on the Jordan his place of abode" (Olshausen, I. 259; Luke i. 80, iii. 2). No reason can be assigned why he should go elsewhere. This was his abode, and where he lived there he preached, and where he preached there he baptized.

An adequate and a most appropriate reason was in "the *character* of the water. Both Gentile and Jew attached a specially purifying value to *running* water" (Dale, p. 332). The use of running water was required in the Old Testament for purification. "And he shall dip them . . . in the *running* water, and sprinkle the house seven times: and he shall cleanse the house with the blood of the bird, and with the *running* water" (Lev. xiv. 51, 52). Philo, the Jew, says: "It is the custom of nearly all others to *sprinkle* themselves for purification with *pure* water; many with that of the sea, some with that of *rivers*" (332). The Roman high-priest directs the Sabine preparing to worship Diana: "Sprinkle yourself first with the *living* stream. The Tiber flows before you in the bottom of the valley." Ovid: "The hands should be washed with *living* water." Virgil: "Sprinkling the body with *river* water" (333). The general sentiment, the usual custom, and obvious propriety were adequate to lead John to use *pure running* water in his baptism, whose symbolic purity was intended to represent emblematically the purifying influence of the Holy Ghost on the soul.

JOHN III. 23:

"Because there was much water there."

Dr. Carson, p. 476, says: "The reason alleged for John's baptizing in Ænon implies that baptism was immersion"; otherwise "there would have been no need of *much* water." But the quantity of water surely could not have been the reason for going to Ænon to baptize. There was a far greater quantity in the river Jordan, only ten miles away. The true reason is given by the Evangelist. Jesus and John were *both* baptizing in the same vicinity. Both parties were baptizing in the neighborhood of each other —Jesus and his disciples, "and John *also*"—because there were many places for baptizing, so that both could baptize without interference. The expression in the original is in the plural number, ὕδατα πολλά—*many waters*—and it is translated in the plural in all other places (Rev. i.

15, xiv. 2, xvii. 1, xix. 6; see also Ezek. xix. 10; 2 Kings v. 12; Judith vii. 17). The number of places for baptizing, and not the quantity of water, is the reason given; and this reason is not given solely to account for the fact that John was baptizing in that place, but for the fact that *both* parties were baptizing near each other—Jesus and his disciples, "and John *also*." The number of fountains of water afforded facilities for the accommodation of both for the purpose of baptizing, and also for any other uses of the water that need might require. Ambrose says "twelve springs," and his remark that they "must be *besprinkled* by these fountains" (Dale, p. 317) shows that it was not quantity of water or dipping in water that entered into his idea of this baptism.

The abundance of water could not have been the reason for leaving the Jordan and going to Ænon, for there was a greater abundance in the river. The reason is found in the season of the year. It was in the month of April, just after the Jewish Passover, when the river Jordan is full to overflowing, rising above its upper banks, and "bearing on its swelling waters all the unclean things which were the result of a year's accumulation within its wide, extended outer banks," and the waters become impure and unfit to symbolize the spiritual purity in which the very essence of baptism consists. At Ænon springs of pure water abound. The waters of Ænon are described by Oriental travellers as "an assemblage of fountains and pools, . . . springs of the *purest* water, six miles northeast of Jerusalem" (Coleman, pp. 268, 269). The secondary meaning of baptizo, denoting purification, gives a *good and adequate* reason why the baptism was at one time at the Jordan and at another at Ænon. This signification harmonizes all the facts, and gives a solution to all appropriate enquiries.

MATT. III. 16:

"Went up straightway out of the water."

An argument for immersion is drawn from the English translation of the Greek preposition in this verse by the phrase "out of." But the correct translation of this Greek preposition (ἀπό) is *from*. It is translated *from* in the same chapter only a few verses previous. "Who hath warned you to flee *from* [ἀπό] the wrath to come?" (v. 7). The Baptist Version of the New Testament translates it *from*.

It is also translated *from* in Luke iv. 1: "Jesus

... returned *from* [ἀπό] the Jordan." It is translated *from* two hundred and thirty-five times in the first four books of the New Testament, and *out of* only forty-two times. "It occurs in the Gospel by Matthew one hundred and nine times, and is rendered just sixty-five times *from*, and only ten times *out of*" (Theodore, p. 262). Dr. Carson says: "I admit the proper translation of *apo* is *from*, and not *out of*" (p. 126). Professor Stuart says: "I have found no example where the preposition ἀπό is applied to indicate a movement *out of* a liquid into the air" (p. 320).

ACTS VIII. 38:

"Went down both into the water."

In this passage also the preposition is thought by some to favor immersion. But the Greek preposition (εἰς) might with equal propriety be translated *to*. In this very chapter it occurs eleven times, and is translated *into* only once. In all the other places it is translated by some other word. Elsewhere in the New Testament it is translated *to, toward, unto, by, at, on,* and other words. It is translated *to, unto,* two hundred and eighty-five times in the first five books of the New Testament. "The preposition (εἰς) occurs

Baptism with Water. 205

single in the Acts of the Apostles *two hundred and sixty-four times*, and is rendered *into* only *sixty-one* times; and of these *sixty-one* times there are twenty-six in which it might properly be rendered *to* or *toward*. . . . The evidence from this single source is *as seven or eight to one* against the supposition that the inspired writer intended to say that Philip and the eunuch went into the water" (Theodore, p. 281). I will give a few examples of its use. Mark xiii. 3: "He sat upon [εἰς] the Mount of Olives." John xxi. 4: "Jesus stood on [εἰς] the shore." Acts xxvi. 14: "When we were all fallen to [εἰς] the earth." Matt. xxi. 1: "When they drew nigh unto [εἰς] Jerusalem" (not into, for they were two miles distant). John xx. 1, 11: "Cometh early unto [εἰς] the sepulchre [not into], but stood without." John xx. 3-5: "Came to [εἰς] the sepulchre, . . . yet went he not in." John xi. 38: "Jesus cometh to [εἰς] the grave." 2 Kings vi. 4 (Sept.): "When they came to [εἰς] Jordan, they cut down wood." They did not go into the water to cut wood. The wood was on the level strand in the river between the upper and lower banks. Matt. xv. 24: "I am not sent but unto [εἰς] the lost sheep of the house of Israel." We are amply justified in saying of this preposition, as Dr. Carson says of ἀπό: "It would have its meaning fully verified if they had only gone down to the edge of the water" (p. 126). He admits that "εἰς might be used if the advance was only to the margin" (p. 132), and that it "sometimes denotes motion to a place that ends on this side of the object" (p. 135).

ACTS VIII. 39:

"When they were come up out of the water."

On the preposition (ἐκ), translated *out of* in this passage, Dr. Carson relies with more confidence. He says: "It always supposes that the point of departure is within the object" (p. 130). "It never, in a single instance, designates merely *from;* it is always *out of*" (p. 355). This, like many other statements too hastily made, reveals the need of a more thorough investigation of the usage of the Greek prepositions. The statement is not sustained by the facts. Winer, p. 366, says: "It originally denotes issuing *from within*"; but he further says, p. 367: "Sometimes it denotes mere direction *from.*" In his " N. T. Lexicon," Robinson gives the meaning *from,* as well as *out of :* "After words implying motion of any kind . . . *from* any place or object, . . . thus marking the point from which the direction sets

Baptism with Water. 207

off." Alexander Buttmann, "N. T. Gr.," p. 322: "The fundamental signification of ἀπό—viz., departure from the *exterior* of an object—is the prevalent one in the New Testament"; and on p. 326 he says: "Owing to the affinity in signification between ἐκ and ἀπό, it is natural that both should often serve to denote one and the same relation." In John xii. 32 Jesus says: "If I be lifted up *from* [ἐκ] the earth." Here the preposition denotes an "exterior relation." The movement is not from a point *within* the earth, but from a point *on the exterior surface* of the earth; not *out of*, but *from*, the earth. Acts xii. 7: "His chains fell off *from* [ἐκ] his hands." So Prof. Hackett translates, and so the Baptist Version, as also the English Version. Matthew, xxvii. 60, says: "He rolled a great stone to the door of the sepulchre"; and Mark, xv. 46: "Rolled a stone *unto* [ἐπί] the door." When, therefore, John, xx. 1, says: "Mary Magdalene . . . seeth the stone taken away *from* [ἐκ] the sepulchre," the meaning is not that the stone was rolled *out of* the sepulchre—for it had not been rolled *into* the sepulchre—but *unto the door* to bar the entrance. Matt., xxviii. 2, says: "The angel . . . rolled back the stone *from* [ἀπό in composition with the verb] the door." This illustrates what Buttmann says of the affinity of the prepositions ἀπό and ἐκ to denote "departure from the *exterior* of an object." Mark xvi. 3: "Who shall roll us away the stone *from* [ἐκ] the door?" The subject is fully discussed by Dr. Dale ("C. and P. B.," p. 182 seq.)

The word has received a diversity of translation in the English Version. It is translated *from* one hundred and two times in the first five books of the New Testament, and *out of* only seventy-nine. "The word occurs *single* in the Acts of the Apostles *sixty-four* times, and it is translated *out of* only *five* times, and one of the five is where our Version has it, 'were come up out of the water'" (Theodore, p. 282). In addition to all this is the fact adduced by Fairchild ("Baptism," p. 79) that "the Greek writers, when they wished, by the force of the words, to express the idea of going *out of*, usually doubled the preposition ἐκ, placing it before the noun and prefixing it also to the verb." This is peculiarly noticeable in the style of the author of the Book of Acts. No less than "twenty examples" of this double use of ἐκ occur in the Acts. But in Acts viii. 39 the single ἐκ is used. If Luke had intended to express the idea of *out of*, he would not have deviated from his usual mode of expressing that idea.

There is no decisive evidence in the language of the sacred writer in this passage in favor of immersion. Prof. Stuart says: "The preposition ἐκ . . . by no means of necessity implies it," and he translates, "*They went up from the water*" (p. 326).

JOHN III. 25:

"Then there arose a question between some of John's disciples and the Jews about purifying."

The question about "purifying" was a question about "baptizing." Baptizing is the subject of which the Evangelist is discoursing in the verses preceding and following, and therefore including, this passage. To treat this verse as if it were not connected in the course of the narrative with what stands related to it before and after is wholly arbitrary.

Theophylact says: "There was a dispute concerning *baptism* between the disciples of John, moved with rivalry, and a certain Jew. For the Jew placed the claims of Christ before those of John; but the disciples of John gave the precedence to their master's baptism. Disputing concerning purification—*that is, baptism*—they came to their master" (Dr. E. Beecher, p. 214).

Chrysostom: "There was a dispute ... concerning *purification*. For the disciples of John, being jealous of the disciples of Christ, and of Christ himself, when they saw them *baptizing*, began to dispute with those who were *baptized*, as if their own *baptism* was superior" (p. 214).

Hermann Cremer ("Bib.-Theo. Lex. of New Testament Greek," p. 311) says: "The baptism both of John and Jesus is designated *purification* in John iii. 25, by which the connection between it and the ritual process of purification (cf. Ezek. xxxvi. 25) is made evident."

Dr. Dale ("C. and P. B.," p. 355) says that the "purification in John iii. 25 is used in its generic character, to include both the baptism of the Jew— *ceremonial* purifying; and the baptism of repentance—the *spiritual* purification of John."

Dr. J. J. Owen, in his comment on the passage, says: "About purifying—*i.e.*, about the nature and efficacy of baptismal purification."

Alford (in loco) says : " John and our Lord were baptizing near to one another," ... and the "dispute" was "about the relative importance of the two baptisms." Whether the dispute involved a comparison between the baptism of John and the baptism of Jesus, or between the symbol baptism of John and the ceremonial baptism of

Baptism with Water. 211

Judaism, it was, as nearly all Christian interpreters explain it, and as the course of thought in the evangelist requires us to understand it, a dispute about baptism, purification.

THE MODE OF BAPTISM.

The essence of baptism does not consist in the mode in which the baptismal agency is applied, but in the condition effected by the agency. The word baptizo does not express *any act*, either sprinkling, pouring, dipping, or any other act, but in sacred use it expresses a condition of ritual purity emblematical of the spiritual purity of the soul. Sprinkling and pouring, and not dipping the body into water, are the divinely-authorized acts by which ritual baptism, whether ceremonial or symbol, is effected.

1. The act of dipping, putting into water and immediately taking out, is not expressed in Greek by the word baptizo, but by BAPTO. Baptizo, in classic use, does not take out what it puts under water. In the New Testament persons are never put under water for baptism. They are baptized *with* water.

2. Sprinkling was the act which, by command of God, was employed during the whole period of the Hebrew commonwealth, from Moses to

Christ, for applying the ashes of a heifer, sacrificial blood, and pure water to effect ceremonial purification; and this ceremonial purification, in the times of John the Baptist and Christ, was called *baptism*, and had been so called during all the ages in which the Jews had spoken the Greek language. This mode of baptism was in constant, daily use among the people, and had the authority of divine command and universal practice. To this every-day, current use of the word in the common language of the Jewish people we are to go to learn the meaning and mode of baptism rather than to classic Greek. It was not classic but Hellenistic Greek which was the vernacular of the Jewish people.

3. Judaic baptism was a type of Christian baptism; Judaic baptism was the purification of the body from ceremonial defilement, and the baptismal agencies were applied by *sprinkling*. This purification of the body, as a ceremonial effect, was perfect, and was well suited to be, what Paul and the Christian fathers represent it, a type of the purification of the soul by the sprinkling of the blood of Jesus. Christian baptism is the purification of the soul by the Holy Ghost through faith in the blood of Christ, represented in emblem by the baptismal use of pure water.

4. Sprinkling and pouring are the divinely-chosen forms by which the prophetic Scriptures declare that the power of the blood of Christ and the influence of the Holy Ghost in changing the condition of the soul shall be represented in the times of the Gospel dispensation. Thus Isa. lii. 15: "So shall he *sprinkle* many nations." Ezek. xxxvi. 25: "Thus will I *sprinkle* clean water upon you, and ye shall be clean. . . . And I will put my Spirit within you." Joel ii. 28: "I will *pour out* my Spirit upon all flesh." The fulfilment of this prophetic announcement by the POURING OUT of the Spirit in the baptism of Pentecost recognizes the literal act of "pouring out" to effect ritual baptism as the physical basis of this metaphorical language to denote the baptism of the Holy Ghost.

5. The Christian fathers often speak of sprinkling and pouring as acts which effect the condition which is expressed by baptism. Some quotations in illustration are given in the second chapter of this book. The practice of immersion among them did not arise from a belief that baptism consisted in the mere act of immersion, for they did not so believe; but it arose from their great error that water must receive a divine, spiritual quality by the agency of the Holy Ghost

to give it *power* to effect Christian baptism, and that this *power* could be more effectually communicated to the baptized, the more completely the water could come in contact with his person. From this error arose the practice of baptizing men, women, and children naked, and other objectionable observances. The agency of the Holy Ghost, according to the Scriptures, is exerted directly on the soul, *not on the water*. The water not only has in itself no saving efficacy, but it receives no saving virtue from any action of the Holy Ghost upon it. It is a symbol, *and only a symbol*, of the real baptism of the soul by the Holy Spirit of God.

CHAPTER X.

THE BAPTISM OF JESUS.

BAPTISM OF JESUS BY JOHN.

THIRTY years of the life of Jesus had passed. In his home at Nazareth among the green hills of Galilee, far from the Temple and under influences more than human, "the child *grew*, and waxed strong in spirit, filled with wisdom," until, in the full maturity of his powers as the Son of Man, he was ready to enter upon his great mission. The time had come for him to commence his public ministry as the Messiah. A mighty awakening had been produced by the preaching of the Forerunner, and the valley of the Jordan was alive with the multitudes who, from all parts of Palestine, were flocking to his baptism. The great design of John was to prepare the people to receive One who was greater than he. It was for this purpose that he preached the baptism of repentance, and administered the symbol baptism with water to those who accepted his preaching. Jesus now came with the rest,

and made application to John for baptism. The
Baptist felt the incongruity and declined, saying :
" I have need to be baptized of thee, and comest
thou to me?" Jesus and John were cousins, and
it is not unlikely that they had often met in
Jerusalem at the Passovers, and that John was
acquainted with the prophecies which his father,
Zacharias, had uttered concerning Jesus. Although John did not know Jesus as the Messiah,
the sign from heaven indicating him and author-
izing John to proclaim him to the people as such
being not yet given, yet he recognized him as
superior to himself, and as one too pure to need
such a baptism as his. He may have known
what a sinless and holy life Jesus had led at
Nazareth, or he may have now received a super-
natural intimation of the character of this new
candidate for baptism. But Jesus removed his
scruples, saying: "Suffer it to be so now: for
thus it becometh us to fulfil all righteousness."

What was the baptism which Jesus received
from John? He did not receive "the baptism of
John" which "all the people" received. Neither
" the baptism of repentance" which John preached, nor the ritual baptism " with water into repentance" which he administered, was appropriate to the Sinless One. " It is one thing to be

baptized by John, and quite another to receive the 'baptism of John.'" There is a diversity of baptisms. "Baptism is not one," says Ambrose; "there are *many kinds* of baptisms." Johannic baptism differs from Judaic baptism, and Christian baptism differs from each of the other two. Robert Hall, an open-communion Baptist, whose memory will ever live, even to the latest age, wrote on "The Essential Difference between Christian Baptism and the Baptism of John."

The baptism of John was a "baptism of repentance." This baptism was for sinners, but the Lord Jesus Christ was not a sinner. It demanded "repentance," but He who never sinned did not need repentance. It required its subjects to "bring forth fruits meet for repentance"; but the perfect life of "the Holy One and the Just" could sustain no such relation. Others were baptized ",confessing their sins"; Jesus had no sins to confess. The promise of "remission of sins" was given in "the baptism of John." It was a "baptism of repentance into the remission of sins." But so far from receiving "remission of sins," the pure and holy "Lamb of God" was about to enter upon his Messianic work as the sole means of procuring this blessing for those who need it. "The essence of John's ritual baptism is found in its symbolization of purification in the soul through repentance and remission of sin. But in the Lord Jesus there was no basis for such symbolization, and consequently there was no basis for the baptism of John" ("C. and P. B.," p. 28).

It is not needful to discuss, or even enumerate, the different views which have been taken of the object of Christ's baptism. No less than ten different opinions are referred to by Meyer, as quoted by Lange on Matthew (p. 76). The true significance of the personal baptism of Jesus by John is seen in the words of Jesus, "Thus it becometh us to fulfil all righteousness," and in the import given to those words in the events of the subsequent narrative. The baptism of Jesus was his consecration to his peculiar work as the Messiah. It was to prepare the nation to receive him in this capacity that his forerunner was divinely commissioned. This was the significance of the sublime scene that followed his baptism. This was the purport of the opening of the heavens upon his gaze while he was praying on the bank of the river. This was the significance of the descent of the Holy Ghost, who came down through the disparted firmament "in a bodily shape like a dove," and rested upon his head. This, also, was the meaning of that divine voice which came from the rent sky, saying: "This is my beloved Son, in whom I am well pleased." God had "sent forth his Son" to accomplish the work of human redemption. As the house of Aaron were set apart to their typical priesthood before the Advent by appropriate rites, so now, when "the fulness of the time was come," Jesus, the "Great High-Priest," was inaugurated into his office by a rite administered by one chosen of God and fitted by his peculiar training and mission to perform this service. This baptism of Jesus by John was "a covenant baptism." It was a baptism *into his work as Messiah.* "In it there is an announcement of the work of redemption, and a covenant engagement by the Son of God to accomplish it. This announcement and assumption of covenant obligation the Father accepts and declares himself 'well pleased.' The Holy Ghost makes like declaration by descending upon and baptizing the covenanting Son for his amazing work now assumed at Jordan, but 'finished' only on Calvary" (Dale, p. 31).

When Jesus says, "Thus it becometh us to fulfil all righteousness," he does not refer to the work of repentance required of the other subjects of John's baptism, but to *his own* work in his Messianic office. His baptism by John was an appropriate rite, requisite as an induction into the peculiar work which he undertook on behalf of mankind. As Rudolf Stier ("Words of the Lord Jesus") says: "This baptism is the true *beginning point* of that obedience the consummation of which, in the death of the cross, it pretypifies. . . . This baptism is his anointing to that sacrifice for sinners which now first properly begins. He afterwards was baptized with the baptism of death, in which he, as the Lamb of God, bore our guilt." So, also, Bengel says: "He not only undertook, when he came to *baptism*, the task of fulfilling all righteousness (Matt. iii. 15), but he also completed it by pouring out *his blood*."

There is nothing in the narrative of the baptism of Jesus by John that can determine its mode. Neither the current use of the Greek word baptizo in the days of John, nor the use of the Greek preposition in its correct construction, affords any evidence for the theory that the baptism was performed by dipping the person into the water. Undoubtedly it was performed in the usual mode. The turn which Dr. Carson gives to Mark i. 9 is fully considered by Dr. Dale in "Johannic Baptism," pp. 375-406, and shown to be at variance with the true construction of the Greek idiom. (See also "C. and P. B.," p. 425.) The facts are narrated by Matthew, iii. 13, thus: " Then cometh Jesus from Galilee to Jordan unto John, to be baptized of him." To this the statement in Mark i. 9, translated as the true construction requires, corresponds: " Jesus came from Nazareth of Galilee to the Jordan, and was baptized by John" (Dale, p. 377). The word Jordan merely denotes the locality of the baptism.

Much is said by some of the baptism of Jesus as an example to us. But the baptism of Jesus was not designed as a model for us. It was his induction into his Messianic office as our Redeemer. It is in this light that we derive from it the instruction which it was intended to convey

THE BAPTISM OF JESUS BY THE HOLY GHOST.

The baptismal rite by which Jesus was inducted into his office at the river Jordan was attended by a more divine baptism. " Jesus also being baptized, and praying, the heaven was opened, and the Holy Ghost descended . . . upon him." The Spirit assumed a visible form like a dove, and was seen by Jesus gliding with gentle motion down from the skies. " And he saw the

Spirit of God descending like a dove, and lighting upon him." John also was a witness of the descent of the Spirit. " I saw the Spirit descending from heaven, and it abode upon him." This descent of the Spirit was the divinely-appointed sign by which the Baptist was to know that Jesus was the Messiah. " He that sent me to baptize with water, the same said unto me, Upon whom thou shalt see the Spirit descending, and remaining on him, the same is he which baptizeth with the Holy Ghost." Thus, as Lange says: " At his baptism he was baptized with the Holy Ghost." For although " the term baptism is not immediately applied to this transaction," says Dale, " it is very clearly involved in the words" of John ; for the expression, " the same is he which baptizeth with the Holy Ghost," denotes an agency which " is predicated on the previous personal baptism of our Lord by the Holy Ghost" (p. 31).

The need which Jesus had of the baptism of the Spirit arose from the human conditions under which he must perform the work which he had undertaken. In his own unique personality he united the divine and human natures. There is that in the Incarnation, as well as in the Trinity, which baffles every effort to understand. But among the things that are clearly taught is the dependence of the human nature of Christ not only on his divine nature and on the Father, but on the Holy Spirit. It has not always been observed to what an extent the activity of his earthly life is referred in the Scriptures to the Holy Spirit as the guiding and controlling cause. By his incarnation he became subject to all the conditions of humanity in its sinless state. An essential part of his mission was "to present to the world a perfect model of man in his true relations to God." As the model man, exemplifying all that man is in his pure humanity, he was dependent upon the Holy Spirit; and in his whole earthly life "he was inspired, directed, controlled, in thought and feeling, and word and action, by the Spirit of God" ("Bib. Sac.," Vol. XXXI. p. 619).

This involves all the essential elements of a baptism of the Holy Ghost. He lived and acted under the *controlling influence* of the Holy Spirit from the time of his baptism by John. Thus Luke says: "Jesus being full of the Holy Ghost, returned from Jordan, and was led by the Spirit into the wilderness." The complete control of the Holy Spirit over him is seen in the strong language of Mark: "And immediately the Spirit driveth him into the wilderness." The Spirit powerfully bore him along, yet with the full consent of his will. After he had vanquished the tempter, "Jesus returned in the power of the Spirit into Galilee." The divine quality of his teaching is attributed to the same source: "For he whom God hath sent speaketh the words of God; for God giveth not the Spirit by measure unto him."

This baptism was unlimited in continuance as well as in measure. It was a life-long baptism. The Spirit, like a dove, not only "lighted upon him," but "it *abode* upon him," as John says, "descending and *remaining* on him." It was a permanent influence. Jesus continued "in this condition of baptism during all the period in which he was engaged in accomplishing his covenant to 'fulfil all righteousness.'" By this influence he was endued with power in his preaching. "The Spirit of the Lord is upon me, because he hath anointed me to preach the Gospel to the poor, . . . to preach the acceptable year of the Lord" (Luke iv. 18). This was promised in the prophetic word: "And the Spirit of the Lord shall rest upon him, the spirit of wisdom and understanding, the spirit of counsel and might, the spirit of knowledge and the fear of the Lord, and shall make him quick of understanding" (Isa. xi. 2, 3). The miracles of Jesus were wrought by the power of the Spirit: "If I by the Spirit of God cast out devils." It was through the Spirit that he offered up himself as the Lamb of God to make atonement: "Who, through the Eternal Spirit, offered himself without spot to God" (Heb. ix. 14). "This offering was the consummation of that covenant assumed at his baptism by John, when he engaged to fulfil all righteousness" (Dale, p. 32).

The Son of God, in his divine nature, had infinite all-sufficiency in himself. But of his own will as God he assumed human nature, and in his human condition he came under the limitations of humanity. The influence of the Holy Spirit upon his human faculties was an essential condition of the accomplishment of his great undertaking as the Messiah. This endowment of Christ by the Holy Ghost for his peculiar work is declared by Peter: "God anointed Jesus of Nazareth with the Holy Ghost and with power: who went about doing good, and healing all that were oppressed of the devil; for God was with him" (Acts x. 38).

THE BAPTISM OF JESUS ON THE CROSS.

Luke xii. 50: "I have a baptism to be baptized with."

Matthew xx. 22 : " Are ye able to drink of the cup that I shall drink of?"

Mark x. 38 : " Can ye drink of the cup that I drink of? and be baptized with the baptism that I am baptized with?"

The announcement in Luke of this baptism of Jesus was made just after the second Passover following his baptism by John. The second allusion to it, in the enquiry put to the two sons of Zebedee which Matthew and Mark record, was made a few days previous to the fourth Passover, just before his crucifixion. The words in the second part of the enquiry, and of the declaration in reply to the response of the disciples, as given by Mark, are omitted by Matthew in Tischendorf's New Testament (1873). Lange also (" Matthew," p. 362) says that " the words " omitted by Tischendorf " are wanting in the manuscripts B, D, L, Z, and in the Sinaitic manuscript, and in many ancient versions, and in all critical editions. They were in all probability inserted from the parallel passages in Mark x. 38, . 39." According to the genuine original, Matthew speaks only of the cup which Jesus must drink ; Luke speaks only of the baptism which he must receive ; Mark speaks of the cup and the baptism, which sustain to each other the relation of cause and effect. By drinking the cup of suffering Jesus was baptized into death. The sufferings which he endured are figuratively represented by the cup which he drank. The contents of this cup of woe contained the baptizing agency which had power to cause a baptism into death. "The word," says Dale, "is used in its well-understood secondary meaning, expressive of controlling influence." The result upon Jesus of drinking this cup was death. "As he drinks he dies, . . . baptized into penal death, a 'ransom for many'" ("The Cup and the Cross," p. 20).

A very different but unsatisfactory explanation is given of this baptism by those who deny that baptizo has a secondary meaning. Dr. Carson (p. 117) makes an unsuccessful effort to separate the cup from the baptism, making them both "figures as independent and as distinct as if one of them was found in Genesis and the other in Revelation." He says they both represent "the sufferings of Christ"—one as "a cup," the other "as an immersion in water." But there is only one metaphor—the cup; and this is both a suitable and a sufficient emblem of the sufferings of Jesus. To represent the same idea under the additional figure of immersing him in water is wholly incongruous and superfluous. There is no reason for so interpreting it, except in the exigency of an erroneous theory of the signification of the word. Dr. Carson thinks that he must interpret the word in conformity with his theory "*that it always signifies to dip, never expressing anything but mode.*" But the mere act of dipping a person in water—a momentary act of slight and trivial influence—is incompetent to express intense suffering. Dr. Carson shifts the word and substitutes the ambiguous word immerse; and passages of a highly poetic nature are quoted by him and others which speak of "floods," and "waves," and "billows," and "water-spouts." But such outbursts of the imagination do not harmonize with the sober historic style of the record which we have in the narrative of the Crucifixion, and they are especially incongruous by the side of the beautiful and well-chosen metaphor by which Jesus so often represents the atoning sufferings of his approaching death as "the cup" which his Father had given him to drink. There is not a single circumstance in the narrative which suggests a water scene, and the picture of an overwhelming flood in this place is only an exercise of the human fancy. The secondary meaning of baptizo, expressive of controlling influence, gives full significance to the cup. A baptism always corresponds in its nature to the character of the baptizing power. The cup which Jesus drank, from the very nature of its contents, had power to cause his death. It was a cup filled with atoning sufferings. He drank the cup, and was baptized into atoning death.

It is not the mode of baptism which gives importance to the right interpretation of this passage. The baptism of Calvary derives its importance from its character and from its central position among Bible baptisms. "The baptism of the Lord Jesus Christ on the cross is that wondrous central baptism in which all other baptisms of the Bible, whether type or symbol or equivalent baptisms, meet" (Dale, p. 42).

This baptism of Jesus was a death-baptism, caused by drinking the cup of suffering which was given to him. In prospect of this baptism he uttered an exclamation of distress: "I have a baptism to be baptized with; and how am I straitened till it be accomplished!" His question to the two disciples: "Are ye able to drink of the cup that I shall drink of?" plainly shows that it was a cup of suffering. The suffering is involved in both the cup and the baptism. The baptism is the result of the drinking of the cup. Mark conjoins the two as cause and effect: "Can ye drink of the cup that I drink of? and be baptized with the baptism that I am baptized with?" The one follows the other. In direct connection with this baptism, both in Matthew and Mark, Jesus speaks of his death: "Behold, we go up to Jerusalem; and the Son of Man shall be delivered unto the chief priests, and unto the scribes; and they shall condemn him *to death*, and shall deliver him to the Gentiles: and they shall mock him, and shall scourge him, and shall spit upon him, and shall *kill him*." So in the further context of Matthew: "The Son of Man came . . . *to give his life* a ransom for many."

The word *baptizo* by frequent usage is competent to express the idea of putting to death. "The dolphin baptizing *killed* him" (Æsop). "I, baptizing you by sea-waves, will *destroy* you" (Alcibiades). "Baptizing others into the lake," DROWNED them (Heliodorus). "Baptizing him," DROWNED him (Lucian). "Whom it were better to baptize," *to* DROWN (Themistius). The word *baptisma* (baptism) is a noun which, from its Greek formation, expresses *condition*. As the action expressed by the verb baptizo is capable of producing death, so the noun baptisma is capable of expressing the condition of death; and this is the signification which its connection in this place requires.

This baptism is caused by drinking from a cup. Cup-baptisms are among the most frequent baptisms spoken of by Greek writers. "Baptisms by drinking are various in character, yet all marked by *a thorough change of condition, pervaded and controlled by the* CHARACTERISTIC *of the baptizing liquid.* No liquid which cannot thoroughly change the condition of the drinker, and subject him to its characteristic quality, is capable of baptizing" ("C. and P. B.," p. 47). A cup filled with an opiate baptizes into *stupor.* "Whom, by the same drug, having baptized," by drinking from a cup (Achilles Tatius). A cup filled with wine communicates its intoxicating quality to the drinker. "Baptized by unmixed wine," by drinking from a cup (Athenæus). "Baptizing powerfully," by drinking from a cup (Athenæus). "Baptized Alexander," by drinking from a cup (Conon). "Resembles one baptized," by drinking from a cup (Lucian). "Baptized yesterday," by drinking from a cup (Plato). "Baptizing, drank to one another," by drinking from a cup (Plutarch). "Baptized by yesterday's debauch," by drinking from a cup (Plutarch). "A body not baptized," by drinking from a cup (Plutarch). "The body not yet baptized," by drinking from a cup (Plutarch). "The character of these baptisms differs according to the distinctive character of the contents of the cup. . . . In every case there is a powerful, penetrating, pervading, and assimilating influence controlling and thoroughly changing the condition of the drinker. *It is this* RESULT *which makes the* BAPTISM. The specialty of the influence individualizes the baptism. The cup which the Saviour drank was filled with such contents as no other cup had ever been filled with. It was not filled with the woes of simple death, but with penal and atoning death; THEREFORE the baptism consequent upon the drinking was such as never had been and never shall be" ("The Cup and the Cross," p. 22). Jesus had not yet drunk the cup while in the garden of Gethsemane. His agony in the garden was in view of the prospect that rose before him. "O my Father! if it be possible, let this cup pass from me: nevertheless not as I will, but as thou wilt" (Matt. xxvi. 39). "O my Father! if this cup may not pass from me, except I drink it, thy will be done" (v. 42).

"Abba, Father, all things are possible unto thee; take away this cup from me: nevertheless not what I will, but what thou wilt" (Mark xiv. 36). "Father, if thou be willing, remove this cup from me: nevertheless not my will, but thine, be done" (Luke xxii. 42). At a later hour, after his visit by the ministering angel, and after his arrest by the band of Jews, the cup was yet to be drunk. "The cup which my Father hath given me, shall I not drink it?" (John xviii. 11).

"This baptism of our Lord is the only baptism of the New Testament which is represented as effected by drinking from a cup. There is no other baptism which could fitly be so represented. This baptism stands all alone. It was no ordinary death-baptism; it was no martyr death-baptism; it was an atoning death-baptism" ("C. and P. B.," p. 49).

The Patrists identify the cup which Jesus drank with his baptism of blood in his death on the cross.

1. Cyril of Jerusalem: "For the Saviour called martyrdom baptism, saying: 'Can ye drink the cup that I drink?'" (p. 39).

2. Origen: "The baptism of martyrdom is given to us; for so it is called, as is evident: 'Can ye drink the cup which I drink?' or 'Be baptized with the baptism that I am baptized with?'" (p. 42).

3. Chrysostom: "Here calling his cross and death a cup and a baptism" (Conant, p. 129).

4. Petilianus: "Ye make martyrs like unto

Christ whom baptizing blood sprinkles" (Dale, p. 40).

The baptismal virtue is in the quality of the baptizing agency, not in its mode of application.

5. John of Damascus, after describing six baptisms, says: "Seventh, that which is by blood and martyrdom, with which Christ himself was for us baptized, as exceedingly august and blessed" (Conant, p. 131).

6. Cyprian: "Baptized by that most illustrious and greatest baptism of blood concerning which the Lord said that he had another baptism to be baptized with" (Dale, p. 39).

7. Origen: "Christ, whom we follow, shed his blood for our redemption, that we may depart washed by our own blood. For it is the baptism of blood only which can make us more pure than the baptism of water has made us. And this I do not assume, but the Scripture declares, the Lord saying to his disciples: 'I have a baptism to be baptized with that ye know not of. And how am I straitened until it be accomplished!' You see, therefore, that he called the shedding of his blood baptism" (p. 41).

8. Theophylact: "He calls his death a baptism, as being a purification for us all" (Cremer, p. 105).

CHAPTER XI.

THE BAPTISM OF THE HOLY GHOST.

ACTS i. 5: "For John truly baptized with water; but ye shall be baptized with the Holy Ghost not many days hence."

The baptism of Calvary was the consummation of that redemptive work to which Jesus consecrated himself in his covenant-baptism at the Jordan. Baptized into atoning death, rising from that death to a life immortal, and just ready to ascend to the right hand of God above, he renewed the great promise of the new dispensation as a *baptism of the Holy Ghost*. This word, by its remarkable history and the significance which it had attained by the laws of language development, was fitted to be the chosen term to express the result of the various operations of the Holy Spirit on the human soul. In the whole range of its varied usage it is a word of *power;* and in its spiritual import, selected as it is by inspiration to denote the highest forms of blessedness which the Redeemer confers upon man by his own personal work and by the work of his Spirit, it is suited to convey instruction freighted with spiritual efficacy. The baptism of the cross is the source from whence the baptism of the Holy Ghost emanates. Jesus, having accomplished by his death that atoning baptism which was essential in order to procure the baptism of the Holy Ghost, now makes the announcement that this baptism shall soon be given to his waiting disciples.

Without making attempt to develop this subject in full, we will present the following points for consideration:

1. The baptism of the Holy Ghost was *the promise of the Father* which Jesus gave to his disciples.

Jesus thus identifies the baptism with the promise: " Wait for the promise of the Father, which, saith he, ye have heard of me. For John truly baptized with water; but ye shall be baptized with the Holy Ghost. . . . Ye shall receive power, after that the Holy Ghost is come upon you" (Acts i. 4, 5, 8). Of this promise, which, as Jesus reminds them, they had "heard" at a previous interview, Luke (xxiv. 49) thus makes record: "And behold, I send the promise of my Father upon you: but tarry ye in the city of Jerusalem, until ye be endued with power from on high." Before the Crucifixion, our Lord had promised that the Father would send the Holy Ghost in his name (John xiv. 16, 26, xv. 26) ; and the same promise had been given in Messianic prophecy, in which, as Peter declares, the baptism of Pentecost had been foretold: " This is that which was spoken by the prophet Joel: And it shall come to pass in the last days, saith God, I will pour out of my Spirit upon all flesh " (Acts ii. 16, 17). All the wealth of blessedness which there is in the promise of the Spirit, as given in the glowing language of the Hebrew prophets, in the simple but expressive words of Jesus, and in the allusions to it by the apostles, is embodied in the baptism of the Holy Ghost. It is the great promise of the Messianic dispensation.

2. The baptism of the Holy Ghost *is under the dispensation of the Lord Jesus Christ.* The administration of the whole work of redemption is committed to him as the Mediator. An essential part of that work is accomplished by the agency of the Holy Ghost. Jesus sends the Holy Ghost and baptizes by the Holy Ghost. Jesus never administered ritual baptism. That work, which was merely symbolical, he committed to his disciples. But the great and essential work of changing the spiritual condition of the soul he himself accomplishes through the agency of the

Holy Ghost. Matt. iii. 11: "He that cometh after me is mightier than I. . . . He shall baptize you with the Holy Ghost." Mark i. 8: "He shall baptize you with the Holy Ghost." So in Luke iii. 16: "He shall baptize you with the Holy Ghost"; and in John i. 33: "Upon whom thou shalt see the Spirit descending, and remaining on him, the same is he which baptizeth with the Holy Ghost."

This is the great declaration which Jesus recognizes and appropriates to himself in his interview with his disciples before the Ascension. He himself, in giving the promise (John xiv. 26), speaks of "the Holy Ghost, whom the Father will send in my name"; and (xv. 26) "whom I will send unto you from the Father, even the Spirit of truth." When, after his ascension, he began to dispense the Spirit in the pentecostal baptism, Peter says: "Being by the right hand of God exalted, and having received of the Father the promise of the Holy Ghost, he hath shed forth this, which ye now see and hear" (Acts ii. 33). So Paul (Tit. iii. 5, 6) speaks of the "renewing of the Holy Ghost, which he shed on us abundantly through Jesus Christ our Saviour." Jesus Christ was qualified to administer this baptism; for he was himself baptized by the Holy

Ghost " descending, and *remaining* on him," and was thus invested, " without measure," with those spiritual endowments which qualified him for every part of his mediatorial work. The work of dispensing the Holy Ghost is one of transcendent importance, and for this part of his work Jesus was fully endued. The declaration in John i. 33 : " The same is he which baptizeth with the Holy Ghost," in its true interpretation, represents Jesus as " the Baptizer who was himself *in* the Holy Ghost, and, being in the Holy Ghost, was thereby invested with power to baptize *by* the Holy Ghost" (" C. and P. B.," p. 53). Ambrose calls Jesus "the Great Baptizer." He is the baptizer by the Holy Ghost. He is the dispenser of this gift.

3. In effecting this baptism the Holy Ghost is *the divine, personal agent.* " Ye shall be baptized *by* the Holy Ghost" (Dale, p. 73). The Holy Ghost is not the local sphere or passive medium in which this baptism takes place, but *the person by whose agency* the baptism is effected. In the places that speak of the baptism of the Holy Ghost, the Greek preposition ἐν is used, and some translate " in the Holy Ghost." But the preposition in this relation is not used in its primary physical and local signification, denoting

"*an expanse within the bounds of which* anything exists" (Winer, p. 384). The Holy Ghost is not "the element *in* or *within* which the act is performed" (Conant, p. 100). The theory which demands the translation "immersed in the Holy Ghost" limits the Greek preposition to its local signification, and denies that it can denote agency. Dr. Conant says the word baptizo in Acts i. 5 and elsewhere is "construed with the local preposition *in*." Dr. Carson (p. 107) says: "The disciples were immersed *into* the Holy Spirit." This results from the error of making the Holy Spirit the receptive element, thus excluding his personal agency in the baptism.

That the Greek preposition has not only a local but an instrumental signification was sufficiently shown in a previous chapter. There is also abundant evidence that it denotes agency and influence in its usage in connection with the Holy Spirit.

Micah iii. 8: "I am full of power *by* the Spirit of the Lord."

Zech. iv. 6: "Not by might, nor by power, but *by* my Spirit, saith the Lord."

Neh. ix. 30: "*By* thy Spirit in the prophets.'

Mark xii. 36: "David himself said *by* the Holy Ghost"; which means, as Robinson ("N. T. Lex.,"

p. 248) says, "Under the power and influence of the Holy Spirit."

Matthew xxii. 43: "How then doth David in spirit call him Lord?" Buttmann explains this, "Impelled by the Spirit." This eminent scholar says that the Greek "preposition ἐν is very commonly used . . . to designate the *means;* and that not only with things (equiv. to the instrumental dative), but also with persons" ("Gram. of the N. T.," p. 329).

Luke ii. 27: "And he came *by* the Spirit into the Temple"—*i.e.*, led by the Spirit.

Luke iv. 1: "Jesus being full of the Holy Ghost . . . was led *by* the Spirit into the wilderness."

Matthew ix. 34: "He casteth out devils *through* the prince of the devils." Winer gives this as an example of the instrumental use of this preposition with the dative, and says: "Ἐν is so used with personal designations" ("N. T. Gr.," p. 388).

Matthew xii. 27: "If I *by* Beelzebub cast out devils"; xii. 28, "But if I cast out devils *by* the Spirit of God."

Rom. xv. 13: "That ye may abound in hope, *through* the power of the Holy Ghost."

Rom. xv. 16: "Sanctified *by* the Holy Ghost."

1 Cor. xii. 9: "To another faith *by* the same Spirit."

1 Peter i. 12: "Preached the Gospel unto you *with* the Holy Ghost sent down from heaven."

These examples are but specimens selected from a widely-extended usage in which the preposition denotes the *agency* of the person or object to which it stands related. This prepares us for the direct evidence of the actual agency of the Holy Spirit in the baptism under consideration. Evidence of the active energy of the Spirit is found both in the promise and in its fulfilment: "He shall teach you all things" (John xiv. 26). "I send the promise of my Father upon [$\dot{\epsilon}\pi\dot{\iota}$] you: but tarry ye in the city of Jerusalem until ye be endued with power from on high" (Luke xxiv. 49). "Ye shall receive power after that the Holy Ghost is come upon you" (Acts i. 8). "They were all filled with the Holy Ghost, and began to speak with other tongues as the Spirit gave them utterance" (Acts ii. 4). So in the diverse baptisms of the Spirit: "There are diversities of gifts, but the same Spirit. There are diversities of operations, but it is the same God which worketh all in all. To one is given by the Spirit the word of wisdom. . . . All these worketh that one and the self-same Spirit, divid-

The Baptism of the Holy Ghost. 243

ing to every man severally as he will. For by one Spirit we are all baptized into one body". (1 Cor. xii.)

The Holy Ghost is *an active* AGENT, not a receiving element *into* which souls are put by some baptizer. " The Baptist view, *which assigns to Christ the work of putting the souls of men in the Holy Ghost as a quiescent receptacle*, revolutionizes the Gospel scheme. . . . It is not the work of Christ to bring the souls of men to the Holy Ghost, but it is the work of the Holy Ghost to bring the souls of men to Christ" ("Johannic Baptism," p. 178).

The use of the Greek preposition in connection with the baptism of the Holy Ghost is *invariable*, while its use is *variable* in connection with baptism by symbol water. The reason given for this by Dr. Conant, p. 100, is that "the Holy Spirit could less properly be conceived as the mere instrument of an act." This concedes that water is a "mere instrument," and that the Holy Spirit is not. This is true, though not in harmony with the theory, but it gives no explanation of the *variable* use of the preposition in connection with water (see chap. ix. p. 192). Dr. Dale ("C. and P. B.," p. 77) gives a much better reason. The qualification of Jesus to administer the baptism of the Holy Ghost depends on, and is derived from, the Spirit. Jesus, therefore, is *always in* the Spirit and *under his influence.* But the qualification of John to baptize with water did not depend on the water. The water, as the mere instrumental means of ritual baptism, may, therefore, either take or omit the preposition in conformity with the Hebraistic or with the classical character of the style, each of which denotes instrumentality. But the constant relation of Christ to the Holy Spirit, as *in* and *remaining under the influence* of the Spirit, requires expression in every reference to the baptism of the Holy Ghost.

This baptism is ascribed both to Jesus and the Holy Ghost: to Jesus as the more remote author, to the Holy Ghost as the more immediate agent. " Christ and the Holy Ghost are not announced as two independent baptizers, but as most intimately united." It is the intimate union of these two Persons with each other, and their mutual relation, from which the peculiar agency of each in this baptism has its origin.

4. The baptism of the Holy Ghost is *the effect of his agency in changing the condition of the soul.* There is no modal action in the baptism of the Spirit. The modal expression, " I will pour out

my Spirit," in the prophecy which Peter says had its fulfilment in this baptism, is used metaphorically. This metaphorical use had its physical basis in a previous literal use of water by pouring to effect a baptism. The resemblance does not lie between the modal act of pouring, in water-baptism, and the manner in which the Spirit is given: *first*, because baptism does not consist in modal action, but in condition resulting from some competent act or influence; *second*, because an attempt to trace such a resemblance would tend to materialize our view of the influence of the Spirit. But the resemblance which is the foundation of the metaphor consists in the idea common to both—viz., *resultant condition.* The baptism which resulted from pouring water on the altar at Carmel was the cleansing of the altar. The baptismal agency was water, the mode of applying it was by pouring, but the baptism did not consist in the act of pouring, but in the changed condition of the altar. The baptism of the Holy Ghost consists in the changed condition of the soul. All baptisms correspond in their character to the characteristics of the baptismal agencies by which they are effected. Baptism is a change in the condition of its object, the nature of the change being determined by the nature of the baptizing power. The baptism of the Holy Ghost is *a complete and thorough change in the condition of the soul effected by his divine agency.* A person baptized by the Holy Ghost comes under his controlling influence, becomes assimilated to him in character, endued with spiritual power, filled with heavenly peace and joy, and qualified for the service of the Master.

There is a diversity in the influences and operations of the Spirit, and the baptism of the Spirit is characterized by a similar diversity. As there is a variety of baptisms elsewhere—" very many kinds of baptisms," Ambrose says—so there is a variety of baptisms in the work of the Holy Spirit in the soul. The baptism of Pentecost was peculiar both in its special character and in its emblem. The specialty of this baptism consisted in qualifying the Apostles for their mission. All the qualifications which they needed in their work of laying the foundations of Christ's everlasting kingdom were communicated to them by the baptism of the Holy Ghost. The power to speak in foreign languages was one of these qualifications, and the symbol of this power was the " cloven tongues," having a fire-like appearance, which sat upon each of them. They also received new light, and strength, and courage, and other elements of spiritual power. They were baptized "*into the* POWER *of the apostleship*," and this was the source of their eminent success.

The baptism of Cornelius and others by the Holy Ghost at Cæsarea (Acts x. 44, xi. 16) belongs to the same class of baptisms as that of Pentecost, including the power to speak with tongues. But there was a great difference in these two baptisms. "The baptism at Pentecost was a baptism qualifying for the apostleship; this baptism was a baptism qualifying for Christian life, with such special endowment as should convince Peter and others that Gentiles were to be received even as Jews into the Christian Church" (Dale, p. 95). The miraculous powers conferred in these and other baptisms recorded in the Acts were not the whole nor the most important endowments bestowed upon the primitive church. The power of working miracles was not peculiar to the new dispensation, but had often been exercised under the ancient economy. This power was not conferred upon all, and it was withdrawn when its temporary purpose was accomplished.

5. The baptism of the Holy Ghost in all its

variety of blessing, miracles excepted, *was the common privilege of all Christians.* The baptism of Pentecost was not limited to the apostles. This baptism, as Peter teaches, was a fulfilment of the prophecy in Joel: " It shall come to pass in the last days, saith God, I will pour out of my Spirit upon all flesh: and your sons and your daughters shall prophesy. . . . And on my servants and on my handmaidens I will pour out in those days of my Spirit." All the membership were to share in the promised blessing. Were they "all filled with the Holy Ghost" by the pentecostal baptism? It is the duty and privilege of all Christians to " be filled with the Spirit" (Eph. v. 18).

The promise was made to all who should comply with the instructions of the apostle: "Ye shall receive the gift of the Holy Ghost. For the promise is unto you, and to your children, and to all that are afar off, even as many as the Lord our God shall call" (Acts ii. 38, 39). Of the disciples in Antioch of Pisidia the sacred historian says: " And the disciples were filled with joy and with the Holy Ghost" (Acts xiii. 52). In the twelfth chapter of the First Epistle to the Corinthians, in which the apostle treats of the diversified operations of the Spirit of God, he

The Baptism of the Holy Ghost. 249

says: "The manifestation of the Spirit is given to every man to profit withal. . . . For by one Spirit we are all baptized into one body" (1 Cor. xii. 7, 13). These statements include all regenerate persons, all who "by the Holy Ghost call Jesus Lord" (v. 3). The promise of the Holy Ghost is not given to the unregenerate: "Whom the world cannot receive, because it seeth him not, neither knoweth him" (John xiv. 17). Only those who have become Christians receive this gift of promise.

The baptism of the Holy Ghost is sometimes received immediately on conversion. A remarkable and instructive example is that of the late Rev. Charles G. Finney, described on p. 20 of his "Autobiography." Sometimes there is an interval after conversion before the gift is received. The apostles were converted some time before they received the baptism. The twelve disciples whom Paul found at Ephesus (Acts xix. 1–7) had not received it. Paul's enquiry, "Have ye received the Holy Ghost since ye believed?" is sometimes quoted in support of the theory that the baptism of the Spirit is not to be expected until after the duration of some interval of time from the period of conversion. But this is a misapprehension of Paul's meaning. Prof. Hackett,

"Commentary," p. 309, gives the true meaning: "*Did ye receive* [note the aorist] *when ye believed?* The participle refers to the same time as the verb." The enquiry implies that they might have received the Holy Ghost *when they believed.* The passage in Eph. i. 13: "In whom also after that ye believed, ye were sealed with that Holy Spirit of promise," is also quoted in support of the same theory. In both these passages we must "note the aorist" participle if we would get the exact meaning. The use of the aorist participle in the Greek shows that the gift of the Spirit *is conditioned on believing*, but it does not require such an interval of time as to lay the basis of the theory of two distinct and unlike experiences, a first and second conversion. The baptism of the Holy Ghost is sometimes received immediately on conversion, and the very question of Paul was, "Did ye receive the Holy Ghost when ye believed?" Their reply shows one reason why they did not: "We have not so much as heard whether there be any Holy Ghost." They had not received the needful instruction. If suitable instruction were given and the conditions complied with, the gift of the Spirit would more frequently be received at the time of conversion.

6. The baptism of the Holy Ghost *is promised*

The Baptism of the Holy Ghost. 251

to believers in all generations to the end of time. The distinguishing characteristic of the Gospel dispensation in contrast with the one preceding is that it is "the ministration of the Spirit" (2 Cor. iii. 8). This is "the glory that excelleth." The promise is not limited to the primitive age. "I will pray the Father, and he shall give you another Comforter, that he may abide with you for ever" (John xiv. 16). Jesus himself could only remain on earth for a temporary period. But the Holy Ghost, whom Jesus promised to send from the Father, will *abide* permanently with his followers. "Neither pray I for these alone, but for them also which shall believe on me through their word" (xvii. 20). "The last days," in which Peter says the promise, "I will pour out of my Spirit upon all flesh," shall be fulfilled, covers the whole period of the new dispensation from the beginning to the end. Joel gave the prediction in the former days, eight hundred years before "the last days" began. In that former dispensation the prophet Isaiah, in prophetic foresight of the permanence of this great Gospel blessing, says (lix. 21): "As for me, this is my covenant with them, saith the Lord: My Spirit that is upon thee, and my words which I have put in thy mouth, shall not depart out of thy mouth, nor out of the mouth of thy seed, nor out of the mouth of thy seed's seed, saith the Lord, from henceforth and for ever." The promise is to Christians of this generation, and will be to those of every generation to come.

7. The baptism of the Holy Ghost is *received by faith*. "Christ hath redeemed us . . . that we might receive the promise of the Spirit through faith. . . . That the promise by faith of Jesus Christ might be given to them that believe" (Gal. iii. 13, 14, 22). This corresponds with the promise as given by the Lord Jesus in John vii. 37, 38: "In the last day, that great day of the feast, Jesus stood and cried, saying, If any man thirst, let him come unto me and drink. He that believeth on me, as the Scripture hath said, out of his belly shall flow rivers of living water." The meaning of this John thus explains to his readers: "But this spake he of the Spirit, which they that believe on him should receive: for the Holy Ghost was not yet given; because that Jesus was not yet glorified." This, as Tholuck remarks, "designates something more than the comparative *amount* of activity and power. It denotes a distinction in the *character* of the outpouring" (Owen in loco).

The baptism of Calvary furnished the superior

conditions which were essential to the baptism of the Holy Ghost in its fulness, variety, and power. The Redeemer, exalted, glorified, enthroned in light and dominion on high, sends the Spirit of truth into hearts prepared to receive him; and this glorious Spirit comes into the soul, and to its admiring view reveals Christ in his beauty, in his love, in his power to save, in his all-sufficient grace. The Holy Ghost reveals Christ to the spiritual apprehension of the believer—Christ in his wonderful person, in the excellency of his character, in the amazing work of atonement by which he secured the everlasting redemption of all who come into a living union with him. The baptism of the Spirit gives light, and life, and joy, and strength to the soul. It gives to the believer *soul-transforming views of Gospel truth, and thus endues him with divine and spiritual power.*

But no one can take in all Bible truth at one view. The views of persons will vary according to their capacities, their degrees of knowledge, the special truths they contemplate, the vividness of their attention, and the degrees of their faith. "There are diversities of operations" also; and "all these worketh that one and the self-same Spirit, dividing to every man severally as he will" (1 Cor. xii. 11). The baptisms of the Spirit are, therefore, *diverse*, both in degree and in the special endowments by which different persons are qualified for different purposes and services. But each believer may receive in full the baptism which he especially needs for his life-work in his own appropriate sphere which an all-wise Providence has assigned him.

8. The baptism of the Holy Ghost *is a blessing to be sought by all Christians.* There is reason to apprehend that the promise of the Spirit is not prized by many according to its value; by some not even understood. The regeneration of the soul by the Spirit of God is not the whole of his work. There are "exceeding great and precious promises" to the believer which he is expected to appreciate and seek for as taught in the Scriptures. The work of the Holy Spirit has always been held in high estimation by those who have had much experience of his influence in the soul. It is the privilege and the duty of all to advance beyond the mere elements, and to seek and receive the fulness of blessing which is comprehended in the promise. Those who would seek and obtain this blessing must comply with the conditions of its attainment.

One of these conditions is a *desire* for the

The Baptism of the Holy Ghost. 255

promised blessing. It would be most irrational to suppose that God would confer such a gift on those who have no desire for it and feel no need of it. The desire for it must be *real* and *strong*. The gift is one of inestimable value, and has been procured at an infinite expense. In order to appreciate its worth we should study with great diligence the teachings of the Scripture respecting the person and work of the Holy Spirit, and by this divine and spiritual knowledge we shall not only attain a true understanding of the promise, but perceive its desirableness, its superlative excellency, and the blessedness which it confers upon those who receive it.

Another condition on which the fulfilment of the promise depends is *prayer*. It was after the ten days of united and earnest prayer that the primitive disciples received the pentecostal baptism. Our Saviour gives both the condition and the encouragement for prayer when he says (Luke xi. 13): "How much more shall your Heavenly Father give the Holy Spirit to them that ask him?"

Another condition is *faith*. As God gives us the fullest assurance in the Bible that the bestowment of the blessings of this promise is "according to his will," we are to ask for it, expecting to receive that for which we pray. We are to receive the promise with a confidence which excludes all doubt. The time, the manner, and the measure of the baptism which Christ by his Spirit will confer, will depend upon his superior wisdom. We must be in a right state of mind to receive it. But of his willingness, and power, and purpose to bestow this blessing upon any Christian who seeks it with strongly-awakened desire, genuine faith, and earnest, persevering prayer, we are to entertain no doubt. The *veracity of God* is the ground of our confidence.

It is implied in what has already been said that *a disposition receptive of the Spirit* is a part of that condition of mind which invites his incoming and indwelling in the soul. All that tends to " grieve the Holy Spirit of God " must be avoided. He is a personal agent, and comes to exert his purifying energy as " the Spirit of holiness." If the believer receives him in a spirit corresponding to the object of his coming, and yields himself up completely to his control, he will dwell with him as his divine Friend, Comforter, and Guide, and bestow upon him the fulness of blessing comprised in the promise.

The most comprehensive expression of the condition of receiving the promise which the

Apostle Peter gives is in Acts v. 32, where he speaks of "the Holy Ghost, whom God hath given to them that obey him." As the baptism of the Spirit is given to the believer, not only to fill his soul with purity, peace, joy, hope, and all spiritual affections and Christian graces, but to qualify him also for his life-work in the service of the Master; and as this spiritual work is of eminent importance in the Christian field, the Christian who seeks and receives in any measure the promise of the Spirit should hold himself in readiness for any Christian work which the Lord Jesus may give him to do. This heavenly baptism involves on his part a complete consecration of himself to God, and in this new condition he belongs wholly to Jesus. The will of the Lord Jesus is his supreme law, and obedience to him will for evermore be his choice, his employment, his honor and joy.

CHAPTER XII.

BAPTISM INTO CHRIST.

ONE of the improvements in translation which Dr. Philip Schaff recommends in his introduction to "The Revision of the English Version of the New Testament" is in Matt. xxviii. 19, which should read, "Baptizing them *into* the name." He says that the "false rendering, '*in* the name,' arose from the Vulgate (*in nomine;* Tertullian had it correctly *in nomen*)." Alford and others agree with Dr. Schaff that in all similar passages the Greek preposition εἰς should be translated *into*.

It is very unsatisfactory to find this Greek preposition, when it follows the Greek verb baptizo in grammatical construction, sometimes translated "for," sometimes "in," then "into," and again "unto." Neither do the commentators give any more satisfaction by their varying explanations, "Into the belief of," "Into the acknowledgment of," "Into the profession of," "In order to," "In reference to," "By the authority of," "In obligation unto," etc., especially as none of these ideas are in the language of the original. Neither is it by any means unimportant to ascertain the exact and true meaning. Well does the *Baptist Quarterly* say: "*A doctrine of grace may dwell in the right understanding of a single preposition.* Who can measure the significance and worth of this one expression of the New Testament, IN CHRIST?" Of equal significance and worth is the expression, "BAPTIZED INTO CHRIST."

Nor are we to despair of coming to a right understanding of its meaning. "Truth is the daughter of time." It must be sought by earnest, patient, and persevering search. The method of Dale, who develops the meaning of this preposition in its connection with baptizo ($\beta\alpha\pi\tau i\zeta\omega$ $\varepsilon i\varsigma$) by an exhaustive investigation of its usage, has led to a result that is rich in spiritual meaning, as well as conformed to the great law of interpretation that "Use is the sole arbiter of language."

There is a physical basis for all the spiritual language of the Bible. There is a literal, primary meaning of words, from which the higher and secondary meanings arise; and this growth of the secondary meanings from the primary can generally be traced, although the difference be as great as the difference between the two spheres, the physical and the spiritual, in which they are found. The word baptizo in connection with the preposition *eis* is a good illustration of this truth; and in tracing its growth by the laws of language development we gain an insight into its profound and affluent significance which will well repay the effort to understand it.

The baptism denoted by the expression, "baptized into Christ," has the same form of words to represent it as the baptism denoted by the expression, "baptized into water." The expression, "baptized *into water*," does not occur in the New Testament, nor any other form of words equivalent to it. But this expression often occurs in classic Greek to denote *the passage of an object into water without return*. This physical baptism in the secular sphere carries its object into the water and leaves it there. The higher and spiritual baptism is a baptism into Christ. The difference between these two baptisms is as great as the difference between Christ and water, between the influence of Christ on the human soul and the influence of water on the mortal body. Yet there are resemblances between these two baptisms. There is a resemblance in the verbal expression, "baptized into." In primary, secular baptism this form of words denotes a literal baptism *into water*. The same form of words, by verbal figure, is transferred from the physical to the spiritual sphere to denote baptism into Christ. Similar are the forms of expression, "baptize *into* repentance," "the baptism of repentance *into* the remission of sins." Thus the two classes of baptisms, the physical and the spiritual, greatly as they differ from each other, have the same verbal form of expression, "baptized into," to denote them. In secular baptisms these words have their literal meaning. The receptive element into which the object passes in its baptism is *water*. In spiritual baptism water does not appear. There is no physical receptive element. But by verbal figure the same form of expression is used, and is so used as to designate the special character of diverse baptisms with exact discrimination.

The resemblance between these two classes of baptisms is not confined to the mere form of words by which they are denoted. There is also a resemblance in their interior signification. *There is an element common to both classes of baptisms,* and the tracing of this common element from its origin in primary baptism to its development in secondary baptism gives an instructive and satisfactory view of its spiritual import. This common element, which belongs alike to physical baptisms and to those which are spiritual, is that of INFLUENCE. It consists in the *influence* which baptizing agencies have over the objects which they baptize. The baptizing power has an influence to change the condition and character of its object. This is true in the physical sphere. Ships, animals, human beings, and other objects, remaining under water for a long period, as they do in the Greekly baptisms of classic writers, come under *the controlling influence* of the water, which in the course of time completely changes their condition.

There are Greekly baptisms, also, in which there is no intusposition in water. The objects of baptism are not enveloped in the watery element. There are baptizing agencies which exert a powerful influence over the condition of their objects in a mode totally different from that of immersion. The baptismal agency is drunk from a cup, and when drunk it penetrates the system of the drinker, and exerts upon him a powerful, and sometimes a controlling, influence. The baptizing agencies are numerous and various. The modes by which these agencies are brought to act upon their objects are also very diverse.

Baptism into Christ. 263

The baptisms, or the changes of condition which result, are as diverse as the baptizing agencies are diverse in their nature and power. Sometimes the same baptizing agency causes diverse results, or baptisms, which, by the use of verbal figure, can be distinguished from each other with precision. All baptismal agencies have *influence*, and each has *its own characteristic influence*, over the respective objects which they baptize.

So it is in the spiritual sphere. A soul baptized into Christ comes under THE CONTROLLING INFLUENCE OF CHRIST, and *by that influence is changed in character*. As, also, any object baptized into water *remains IN the water*, so those who are baptized into Christ *remain IN Christ;* and as objects remaining *in the water* are by this their physical baptism *changed* in *their state or condition* by the powerful action of the water over them, so in the superior, spiritual baptism, remaining *in Christ* and under the power of his influence, *the soul is changed in its spiritual condition*, and becomes *assimilated to him in its character*.

A brief illustration of the original and primary use of the expression, "baptized into," will aid in the understanding of its secondary use.

Heliodorus says: "Every form of war was enacted, . . . slaying some on land, and baptizing others, with their boats and huts, into the lake" (Conant, p. 39).

This is one of many examples which illustrate what Dr. Conant says (p. 89)—that "the Greek word is also used where a living being is put under water for the purpose of drowning, and of course is left to perish in the immersing element."

Achilles Tatius says: "And there is a fountain of gold there. They, therefore, baptize *into the water* a pole smeared with pitch. . . . And the pole is to the gold what the hook is to the fish, for it catches it" (p. 40).

The pole prepared with pitch is put into the water in order to catch the particles of gold that are floating in the stream.

Strabo says: "The water solidifies so readily around everything that is baptized *into it* that they draw up salt crowns when they let down a circle of rushes" (p. 29).

Hippocrates, in a medical work, says: "Again baptize it *into* breast-milk" (p. 34).

The design of the prescription was to secure the emollient influence of the milk.

In these and similar examples the object passes into a physical element, water or some other fluid, by the agency of which it undergoes a change. The nature of the change in each case will depend upon the nature of the receptive element under whose influence the object passes. A living being enveloped in water will perish *by suffocation*. A gold-bearing fountain *gilds* the pole immersed in it. Intusposition in milk *makes emollient;* in blood, makes the object *red*. Intusposition in water saturated with salt causes incrustation. Each baptismal agency *imparts its own characteristic quality* to the object which comes under its influence.

The transition from baptisms of this class to those of the secondary class in which the expression "baptized into" is used in verbal figure is natural and easily traced. In the secondary class of baptisms there is no physical receptive element, no intusposition in water, no immersion; but there is an IDEAL *element*, and that ideal element resembles the physical element in the common idea of, *influence*. In primary baptisms the object passes into, and comes under the controlling influence of, some *physical* element. In secondary baptisms the object passes into an *ideal* element, and comes under its controlling influence In other respects the difference between the two classes of baptisms is total and absolute. Two or three examples will be sufficient to illustrate this class of baptisms.

Josephus, describing the condition of Gedaliah at a drinking party, employs this expression: "Baptized into insensibility and sleep by drunkenness" ("Jud. Bap.," p. 92).

The drunkenness of Gedaliah brought him into an insensible condition—a condition of stupor and sleep. There was no physical element into which Gedaliah passed and by which he was enclosed in this baptism; but the condition of insensibility and sleep into which he passed is expressed in a form of language borrowed from physical baptisms. As a man baptized into water comes under the controlling influence of the water as a receptive element, so a man baptized into stupor and sleep comes under the controlling influence of stupor and sleep as the ideal element. The resemblance is in the common idea of *influence* which belongs to both the physical and the ideal elements. In the one class of examples the object passes into a *physical*, fluid element, and comes under its control; in the other class the object passes into an *ideal* element, and comes under its control.

Another example occurs in Clemens Alexandrinus: "Baptized by drunkenness into sleep" ("Johannic Baptism," p. 261).

In this, as in the preceding, example, "drunkenness" is the baptizing power, and "sleep" is the verbal element denoting the condition into which, and under the influence of which, the object passes.

The nature of a baptism is always determined by the nature of the baptizing power. Good instruction can baptize into a condition of mental purity. "Baptized by the word of doctrine" (p. 201), says Basil. In like manner bad instruction can baptize into a condition of vice. Thus Clemens Alexandrinus says of a certain class of teachers: "Teaching the practice of pleasure and passion, they baptize *out* of chastity *into* fornication" (p. 261).

These quotations are sufficient to illustrate this usage. There is no literal, physical, fluid element into which the object passes, but there is an ideal element, denoting by verbal figure *the condition into which the object comes* as the effect of the baptizing power.

There is a special advantage in this use of verbal figure to denote the ideal element in this class of baptisms. It furnishes a form of words by which the different baptisms caused by different baptismal agencies can be distinguished from each other with exact discrimination. Sometimes the same baptizing power is capable of producing different conditions, or baptisms. In all these cases the nature of the baptism can be known from the nature of the ideal element which is represented, in verbal figure, by the words "baptized into." Thus, while wine produces only one specific effect on the drinker— viz., a wine-baptism, or drunkenness—the effects of drunkenness are greatly diversified. And since drunkenness, according to Josephus and Clement, is a baptizing power, the baptisms caused by drunkenness may be diverse. But this verbal figure furnishes an admirable form of words to define and limit these diverse baptisms. Drunkenness can not only baptize into insensibility and sleep, but it can baptize into poverty, into shame, into crime, into despair, into destruction, and each of these diverse conditions can be designated with precision by the use of this verbal figure. Belshazzar, the King of Babylon, by his iniquity was baptized into terror, into misery, into destruction (Isa. xxi. 4. Sept.) If these various specific results of a single baptizing agency can be thus distinguished from each other by this verbal figure, with equal power of discrimination the same verbal figure can designate the different baptisms which result from different agencies.

"BAPTIZED INTO MOSES."

This verbal figure is often used in the New Testament and by the Christian fathers, and serves to give the most definite and complete expression to the thought. Paul says: "Our fathers . . . were all baptized into Moses" (1 Cor. x. 2). The baptism was not *into water*, but *into Moses*. The expression exactly defines and limits the baptism. They were baptized *into* MOSES, *not into Pharaoh*. By this baptism the Israelites were delivered from the power and dominion of the Egyptian king, and brought into subjection to Moses. This baptism into Moses brought them into complete subjection to his control. The nature of the baptism consisted in the nature of the influence which Moses had over the nation as their leader. The expression, "baptized into Moses," denotes the fulness and completeness of the devotion of the Israelites to Moses as their divinely-appointed leader to the promised land. The whole nation were baptized into Moses, and this baptism gave him a complete and controlling influence over them, and they were willing to follow him into the great and terrible wilderness. Before this baptism they were fearful, distrustful, insubmissive, and almost ready to go back and "serve the Egyptians." But in their baptism their whole condition and attitude towards Moses were changed. There was no "definite act" in this baptism, nor did the nation pass into any physical receptive element. But they did pass into a condition of subjection to the influence of Moses, and this is very happily expressed in the verbal form of an ideal element which defines with precision the thought which was meant to be conveyed.

"BAPTIZED INTO JOSHUA."

The Patrists, in like manner, employ this form of expression. Origen, referring to 1 Cor. x. 2, "baptized into Moses," says: "So, also, it may be said of Joshua, that all were baptized into Joshua by the Holy Spirit and water" "Jud. Bap.," p. 321).

They were not baptized *into the water.* They were baptized into Joshua *by* the water, or, as Origen says in other places, "by the Jordan," "*by the Spirit and the river.*" The Holy Spirit and the water of the river were the *agencies* by which the baptism *into Joshua* was effected. There was no immersion in this baptism. The water of the river below the crossing flowed away to the Dead Sea, the water above "rose up upon an heap," and "all the Israelites passed over *on dry ground.*" The very object of the miracle was to keep them out of the water. The whole narrative absolutely excludes the idea of "a definite act"—dipping a nation of people into the water. They were made willing to follow Joshua as their leader by the influence of the miracle and of the Holy Spirit. They were baptized *into Joshua.* It is impossible to explain this as a literal baptism. The Israelites were not put into Joshua as into a receptacle, or into a physical element, like water. Two millions of people cannot be literally put into one man. But by verbal figure this form of words expresses the subjection of the Israelites to Joshua as their leader. There is no resemblance whatever between the mode of this baptism and any mode of literal baptism. But there is an instructive resemblance in relation to *the source of the influence* in the two classes of baptisms. In one class of those physical baptisms which are denoted by the expression "baptized into," the design is to develop *the characteristic quality* of the enveloping element over the object which it encloses. "They baptize a pole into the water" to develop the gold-bearing quality of the water, and cover the pole with gold particles; "baptizing others into the lake" to subject them to the suffocating influence of the water and drown them; "baptize it into milk" to develop the emollient quality of the milk; the salt quality of the water, of which Strabo speaks, encrusts with salt the circle of rushes "baptized into it," so that they draw up salt crowns. In all these and similar examples the intusposition in water or other fluid is for the sake of securing the influence of the investing element over the baptized object.

So in the class of baptisms in which there is no intusposition in a physical element, but where the influence of an ideal element is secured, the source of that influence is expressed by verbal figure in the same form of words. Thus Origen says the Israelites "were all baptized into Joshua." They were devoted to him as their leader, and came under his direction and control. Their whole condition and character were modified and changed by the kind of influence which Joshua exerted over them. This subjection to the influence of Joshua as their leader was the baptism of Israel at the river Jordan.

GAL. III. 27:

"For as many of you as have been baptized into Christ have put on Christ."

The exposition of this and similar passages in conformity with the principle that "usage gives law to language" will develop its true meaning. The meaning is clearly seen from the illustrations which have already been given of the use of the form of verbal figure which appears in the important expression, "baptized unto Christ."

We have already seen that a *person* may be introduced, by verbal figure, as the *ideal* receptive element in a baptism. We have also seen that the nature of the receptive element determines the nature of the baptism. The baptism of this passage has in it nothing peculiar except the character of the person, which determines the character of the baptism.

As there was a baptism *into Moses* and *into Joshua*, so there is a baptism *into Christ*. Moses was a type of Christ, and Joshua another. As the baptism of Israel into Moses was their subjection to the special authority and guidance of Moses, and as their baptism into Joshua was their subjection to the special control and leadership of Joshua, so is baptism into Christ a subjection to the special influence of Christ as Saviour and Lord. The expression, rightly understood, has a meaning weighty and profound. It denotes the full, peculiar, and controlling influence which Christ exerts on those who by the Holy Ghost are baptized into him. By their baptism into Christ they come under the power which he has to change their spiritual nature and to assimilate their character to his own. All baptizing agencies have an assimilating power by which they communicate each its own characteristic quality to the baptized object. Those who are baptized into Christ receive from him his own characteristic and transforming influence. Christ enstamps upon the soul his own bright image. Baptized into Christ, the soul becomes like him in its spiritual dispositions and in its new and heavenly virtues. It is a regenerative baptism through the agency of the Holy Ghost uniting the soul to Christ.

This is not ritual baptism. The very terms in which the apostle describes it exclude the external and declare the internal and spiritual: "As many of you as have been baptized into Christ *have put on Christ.*" This is something more profound than an outward rite or an external profession. To put on any one, by universal usage, meant an assumption of his character. To put on Christ is to be clothed with the garment of his virtues as the dress of the soul. He who is clothed with Christ is invested with "*the robe of* RIGHTEOUSNESS." The whole chapter treats of union with Christ by faith through the Spirit of God. He who puts on Christ becomes Christ-like. His likeness to Christ in character becomes such that what Christ is, is seen in all his conduct. This investiture of the soul with the character of Christ is the baptism into Christ.

ACTS VIII. 16:

"They were baptized into [εἰς] the name of the Lord Jesus."

The use of a different formula of baptism by the apostles from the one given in Matt. xxviii. 19 is remarkable, but no mode of accounting for it has ever proved satisfactory. The exposition of Matt. xxviii. 19 by Dr. Dale makes the whole subject clear and consistent, and will attract the attention of Christian scholars. The meaning which he develops is sustained by strong reasons and is very interesting, but the subject lies beyond the scope of this book. But in the formula which the apostles used the translation of the preposition, *into*, is the one which gives the true meaning. It is always translated "into" by Dr. Conant in its classic usage, and most other recent scholars so translate it in the New Testament. In Acts x. 48, "Baptized in the name of the Lord," the Greek preposition ἐν is used, and signifies *by the authority of the Lord*. In Acts ii. 38, "In the name of Jesus Christ," the Greek preposition ἐπί is used, denoting *the reliance upon Christ* in which the nature of faith consists. These three different forms of expression in the Greek of the inspired writers have different meanings, and these different meanings ought to be kept clear and distinct. The Greek expression βαπτίζω εἰς is an organic phrase, and should always be translated *baptize into*. In all cases, by universal consent of scholars, in physical baptism, where this expression occurs, the object *passes into the water* or other element. And where there is no intusposition in water or other physical element, but where the element into which the object (verbally) passes is *ideal*, Dr. Conant, in his translations outside of the Scriptures, is in accord with all other scholars in translating the preposition "*into*." *Usage gives law to language;* and in the New Testament conformity to this law and consistency of interpretation both require the translation *into* when the preposition follows baptizo in grammatical construction. When it follows other words, the usage is often different.

But what is the signification of the expression, "baptized into the name of the Lord Jesus"? The *name* of the Lord Jesus denotes his whole person, character, and work as the REDEEMER, *the Incarnate Son of God*. The expression, "baptized INTO the name," presents "the name of the Lord Jesus," by verbal figure, as the *ideal element* into which, and under the influence of which, the baptized person comes. The character of the baptism is known from the character of the receptive element, which in this instance is not physical but ideal. The baptism of the soul by the Holy Ghost into the name of the Lord Jesus introduces the soul into *a oneness with Christ*, and secures his controlling influence over the soul, thoroughly changing its spiritual condition into a state of harmony with him. This internal and spiritual baptism is symbolized by an external rite. Christian baptism is twofold—*real* in the soul, and *ritual* in the emblem. "The ritual baptism of Christianity has no independent existence as a baptism. It is solely the adumbration of the baptism of the Holy Ghost. They are not two baptisms, the one spiritual and the other physical, but 'one baptism,' the former real, the latter ritual, symbol of the real." The mere external rite has in itself no efficacy, and is but an empty form. But in its true relation to the baptism of the soul by the Holy Ghost it has the significance and power of a symbol. This symbol power does not consist in the mere act, but in the purifying quality of the water, which renders it a suitable emblem of the purification of the soul by the Holy Ghost.

ACTS XIX. 5:

"They were baptized into the name of the Lord Jesus."

This, like the preceding, is an example of ritual baptism. Paul found twelve disciples of John the Baptist at Ephesus. Finding them lacking in Christian knowledge and the gift of the Holy Ghost, he enquired: "Into what [baptism] then were ye baptized?" They replied: "Into John's baptism." The baptism which John administered is expressed by the ritual formula, "I baptize, with water, into repentance." The baptism which he preached was "the baptism of repentance into the remission of sins." The rite which he administered was "a symbol of the purification of the soul consequent upon repentance. . . . The baptism '*into repentance*' was not the sole or ultimate baptism to be received, but was only antecedent to another baptism inseparable from it, namely, 'into the remission of sins'—the strongest possible expression declarative of a condition in which there was complete pardon of sin" (Dale).

The baptism of John derived all its efficacy from *the Lamb of God*, for whose coming it prepared the way. The baptism of Christianity included all that was valuable in John's baptism, and it superadded blessings immeasurably superior. *The name of the Lord Jesus* is the source whence come the remission of sins and all other spiritual blessings. Into his name, therefore, the twelve were baptized, and "the Holy Ghost came on them."

The ritual baptism of John and the ritual baptism of Christianity was not a baptism *into water*, but a baptism *with water*. Water never appears in the New Testament as the receptive element, but always as the instrumental agency. The two examples of ritual baptism just noticed present the name of the Lord Jesus as the ideal element, but say nothing of the mode of using the water. The sacred historian, in speaking of the use of symbol water in baptism, employs the dative without the preposition—Luke iii. 16, Acts i. 5, xi. 16—denoting the *element* WITH *which* the rite was performed. This was doubtless its use in these and all other examples of ritual baptism.

ROMANS VI. 3:

"Know ye not that so many of us as were baptized into Jesus Christ were baptized into his death?"

Baptism into the death of Jesus Christ is baptism into Christ in his special character as dying on the cross for our redemption. The special and definite nature of this baptism is expressed with discrimination and precision by the use of the verbal figure, "baptized into his death." Like other baptisms of the same class, the character of this baptism is known from the character of the ideal element. The ideal element in this baptism is the death of Jesus Christ; and as his death has an atoning efficacy, those baptized into his death receive the characteristic influence which his atoning death has power to exert. The death of Christ has a sin-remitting power and a soul-purifying power, and those who, by baptism into his death, come under its influence, are thoroughly changed in their spiritual condition. This is the reason why they become, as Paul says, "dead to sin," and "live therein no longer." It is the power of this baptism which produces this spiritual effect. No external rite can accomplish such a result.

This is not ritual baptism. There is nothing in the language or in the thought that denotes the external rite. There is no administration of the rite, no description of the rite, no exposition of the rite, no circumstance that relates to the rite. There is nothing external in this baptism.

The whole theme of discourse relates to the condition of the soul, the power of the Gospel to change its character, so that it shall become dead to sin and continue therein no longer, but, in spiritual union with Christ, live a new life.

The nature of this baptism is specified and defined so as to make it definite and distinct. The form of expression which, by verbal figure, represents *the death* of Jesus Christ as the ideal element in this baptism, designates its special character, and distinguishes it from every other baptism with the most exact discrimination. The baptism is not *into water*. This physical baptism is not only not named by the apostle, but it is excluded by the totally different baptism which he specifies and describes. The receptive element is not water or any physical element, but the baptism is *into the death of Jesus Christ*, and THIS is what *marks its character* and gives it its *spiritual import*.

The baptism is internal and spiritual in its nature; and this internal and spiritual baptism alone is capable of meeting the demand of the apostle's argument. Paul was a good reasoner; and when he undertakes to refute the objection that his doctrine of grace leads men to continue in sin, we have a right to expect a *valid* reason. He adduces the fact that we are "baptized into the death of Christ," as Augustine says, "*to* PROVE that we are dead to sin." The external rite, in whatever form administered, cannot prove this, as millions of examples of the failure of the external rite to promote holiness attest. No external profession can prove it. The internal and spiritual baptism alone can ensure that holy living which the cogency and validity of the apostle's argument require. It is the spiritual efficacy of this baptism that renders the argument of the apostle conclusive, and gives it its triumph.

ROM. VI. 4:

"Therefore we are buried with him by baptism into death."

Into what death? Not death in general, but *the death of Jesus Christ*. The definite article before the word "death" in the Greek (τὸν θάνατον) designates a particular death — the death just spoken of, "*his death*." The definite article before the word "baptism' in the Greek also indicates a particular baptism — viz., the baptism spoken of in the previous verse, "baptized into his death." The preposition "into" marks the relation of "the death" to "the baptism," "the baptism into his death." It is not "buried into death," as some, not observing the grammatical construction, erroneously represent, but "by baptism into *his* death we are buried *with him*." Jesus was buried in a rock sepulchre. We are buried WITH HIM, *not in water, but in the tomb of Calvary*. Christ was (literally) crucified and buried. We are crucified and buried with him (figuratively) by union with him. Through faith in his atoning death—"baptized into his death"— we receive the special influences and blessings which that death has power to impart. The phrase, "buried with him," merely carries out and intensifies the thought. The burial of Christ was the fit sequel to his death. They who are crucified with Christ are, by the congruity of the metaphor, buried with him, as they are also risen with him.

COL. II. 12:

"Buried with him in baptism."

Translating the Greek article before "baptism," and supplying the ellipsis from Rom. vi. 4, it will read, "Buried with him in the baptism" (into his death). The sentiment is the same in both places.

The internal and spiritual meaning of this passage is made clear and certain by its connection with the previous verse. The burial with Christ in baptism is the circumcision of Christ, which is spiritual, "made without hands," a change of spiritual condition, a renovation of character, "putting off the body of the sins of the flesh by the circumcision of Christ: buried with him in baptism." The Patrists identify "the circumcision of Christ" and "the burial with him in baptism" as one and the same thing, and spiritual in signification. (See Chap. II., p. 61.)

The spiritual nature of the baptism is also indicated in the English version of what follows, which comprises *faith* as an essential constituent in the baptism: "Wherein also ye are risen with him through the faith of the operation of God." Prof. Stuart translates: "Ye have risen with him [Christ], by faith WROUGHT BY the power of God," and says: "Here, there is a *resurrection by faith—i.e.,* a *spiritual, moral* one" (p. 329). The translation of Tyndale is the same. Olshausen says that "all the later interpreters are unanimous on the point that the meaning is, 'faith which the operation of God calls forth.'"

Some who see and admit that "the leading, underlying thought is death to sin, and spiritual resurrection to newness of life," and that "the apostle may have intended simply to intensify the thought by adding 'buried with him in baptism,'" yet think "that the thought in the figurative or spiritual is drawn from the ACTION of the *literal* and *material*" ("C. and P. B.," p. 263). To this Dale replies: "There is no '*the* ACTION' belonging to baptizo. The acts which meet the demand of this word are diverse and contrary, and therefore cannot be expressed by it." His four volumes are full of the evidence that the word does not express a definite act, but *condition* resulting from *any* act or influence competent to effect the condition.

The literal and material *is the* BASIS of the figurative and spiritual. But, as we have seen, this literal and material basis is not found in the Scriptures, but in classic Greek; and there, *not in a momentary act, to dip, but in a condition of intusposition of* UNLIMITED CONTINUANCE. This is what gives to the receptive element in literal, primary baptism its controlling influence over the object which it encloses. To this the vital thought in secondary, spiritual baptism corresponds. This is what gives special significance to the baptism into the death of Jesus Christ. This is what gives to this baptism its meaning, life, and power. Those who are baptized *into the death* of Jesus Christ, buried *with him* by the baptism *into* HIS DEATH, come under its full, special, and soul-transforming POWER. They receive into their souls its sin-remitting and its spiritually purifying influence. The death of Christ has an atoning, life-giving, redeeming efficacy, and he communicates this divine influence to those who by the Holy Ghost are baptized into him. As in primary baptism baptizo does not take out what it puts in, so in this spiritual baptism "*the* SOUL *is not taken out of the baptism* into which it is baptized." Being baptized into Christ, *it remains in Christ*, and continues in sin no longer. There is a wealth of profound and precious meaning in that expression which we meet with so often in the New Testament, IN CHRIST. Into this blissful and lasting condition we come by BAPTISM INTO CHRIST. Out of this baptism the soul is never taken, *but continues in it for ever.*